THIRTY-THREE YEARS OF RUNNING IN CIRCLES

RAND MINTZER

ISBN: 978-1-4834-1971-8 (sc)
ISBN: 978-1-4834-1970-1 (e)

Library of Congress Control Number: 2014918266

Lulu Publishing Services rev. date: 11/04/2014

CONTENTS

DEDICATION

"They say behind every great man is a woman. While I am not a great man, there's a great woman behind me."
Meryll Frost,
Most Courageous Athlete 1945

Like Mr. Frost, I am not a great man. Unlike Mr. Frost, there are several great women behind me:

My mother, Carole Koppel, my grandmother, the late Margaret Ross, my high school counselor, Gloria Eickmeyer and my wife Andrea.

I am also blessed with great women in waiting, my daughters Avery and Hayden.

To these six extraordinary women, I would like to dedicate this book.

ACKNOWLEDGEMENTS

First of all to my family who dutifully sat with their eyes glazing over while I read and reread them completed and revised chapters of the book.

I would like to thank the many people who read early drafts of the book and provided invaluable feedback and encouragement. I am thanking them globally because I do not want to forget anyone. A special thanks to Jason Luong who discussed this book with me over hundreds of miles on our long Saturday runs which always started way too early in the morning for him.

A thank you to two of my editors, Pat Cuchens and my oldest daughter Avery.

A special thank you to my friends Zack Fertitta and Rick Marai who convinced me that the book was worthy of publication.

I remain in awe that many pillars of the running community would give so freely of their time, John Bingham, Rich Benyo, Drew Prisner and Andy Yelanak. A special nod to Jeff Galloway who not only helped with this book but for almost a decade has answered every running question I have sent him.

Thank you to my Galloway Group the Road Warriors for providing me with hours of good company on more runs than I can count. A thank you to the Marathon Maniacs for granting me membership to their outstanding organization.

Finally, this book would not have been possible without the cast and crew of *See How She Runs*, and Byron Wood.

FOREWORD – 33 YEARS OF RUNNING IN CIRCLES

By Drew Prisner

My name is Drew Prisner, and I am a runner. In fact, I have been running since August, 1987, when a chance encounter with the sport at the start of my sophomore year in high school led to a lifelong kinship with the idea of simply putting one foot in front of the other, trying to go farther or faster than I had the day before. Running has been a big part of my life for the majority of my existence, and it has been the impetus for many of my highest highs and lowest lows. Winning the 2002 Houston Marathon was an unbelievable experience I will never forget, nor will I ever forget the spring of 1993, when plantar fasciitis in my right foot precluded the defense of my 3000-meter steeplechase conference championship at my college team's outdoor conference track & field championships. Any runner can tell you that running can be a fickle friend. But there is something addicting and intoxicating about our sport, a hard-to-define quality that makes us come back to it, even when it has caused us to curse it and swear it off in moments of fear, anxiousness, and disappointment. That same quality also causes us to embrace it, defend it, and share its myriad rewards with fellow runners who understand what it is to "run."

I met the author, Rand Mintzer, about five (5) years ago in the Harris County (Texas) Criminal Justice Center. We are both criminal defense lawyers based out of Houston. I can't remember the exact day we met, but I do recall liking Rand from the moment we met. Rand has a warmness about him, and I could tell right away that he was smart, engaging, and disciplined. He is also quite fit, with an outward appearance that belies his true age. I am sure that aspect of his physical appearance caused me, upon meeting him, to surmise that he might be a runner. Nonetheless, over time we discovered that we both share a love of running, and our sport has been the subject of many a conversation with Rand.

I was honored when Rand asked me to write the foreword to his book, *33 Years of Running in Circles*. He emailed the draft for me to read, telling me that his goal was to write a book about running from the point of view of a "middle-of-the-packer," as opposed to many of the running books extant that focus on elite athletes and world-class training methods and theories. He told me that he envisioned it as an interesting book that could be read in one setting, such as on an airplane flight or during a lazy Saturday afternoon. I could tell he was proud of his literary accomplishment, and, upon receiving the draft, I opened up the document on my laptop and began reading.

33 Years of Running in Circles is an engaging tale of the effect that running has had on one man's life. From the beginning of the book, the reader gets the very real sense that Rand is being honest and direct with his audience about his life experiences, whether they be awkward and lacking confidence or successful and triumphant. We get to see Rand as an overweight youth who is struggling to find his place in the world, and later we are exposed to the Rand who will let nothing get in the way of achieving his personal goals. From the farm to Kentucky Fried Chicken, from Jonesboro, Arkansas to Houston, Texas (and everywhere in between), we learn about the author and discover the type of person he was and is – and doubtless will continue to be. Sure, the title of the book is *33 Years of Running in Circles*, but the "running" part of that title is simply a backdrop to the Story of Rand. The sport of running has woven itself into the fabric of the author's life, and it has supplied him with the one constant on which he can lean in an ever-changing and ever-challenging world. For those of us who call ourselves runners, we see ourselves in Rand – ever pushing our physical, mental, and emotional limits, ever jousting at (running) windmills, getting knocked down as a result of injury, disappointment, or burn-out, getting back up to toe the starting line just one more time. This is the arc of the life-long runner, and, if we are honest with ourselves, we wouldn't have it any other way. That's what makes us different, and we should revel in that difference, even if non-runners view us as slightly insane.

If you are a runner – and even if you are not – do yourself a favor and turn to page one (1) of *33 Years of Running in Circles*. You will quickly find yourself on page 95. And your day will be just that much brighter for it.

WHY ANOTHER BOOK ON RUNNING?

Here's my recollection of a conversation with Bruce Glikin at the 2009 Houston Marathon Expo. He is a 2:39-marathoner and the running fiction author of *Slinger Sanchez Running Gun*, *Distant Runner*, and *Hope's Last Run*.

> RM: I read your last book [*Hope's Last Run*] and really enjoyed it.

> BG: Well, thank you. That means a lot to me. It was something different, writing a book from a woman's perspective.

> RM: Have you ever thought about writing a book about an average runner? It seems like you would have a large audience since the majority of runners are average.

> BG: I could not relate to that.

I started writing this book in 2011, and I finally finished it in 2012. With rare exception, the majority of this book was written in the study of my home that I share with my wife and my two daughters. The wall behind me is a bookshelf from top to bottom. I would estimate that the shelves filled to capacity hold somewhere between five hundred and six hundred books. A cursory glance at the books would indicate that at least a third of them are about running and nutrition. I am not taking into account the running books downloaded to my Kindle. I am also not counting the books I have given away—loaned, donated, or sold—to Half Price Books (which is like giving them away, but you get reimbursed for a percentage of the gas you burn driving there) to get money to buy more books about running.

I am now over half a century old. I never even saw a running book until I was in college when Jim Fixx released *The Complete Book of Running*. When I read it, the clouds parted. Through the pages, Jim Fixx was talking to me—Rand Mintzer—a fellow runner. I was even more inspired to embrace my relatively new activity—running. Up until that point in my life, the only other thing I found as profound was the first time I saw the Grateful Dead. I felt that Jerry Garcia's guitar solos were being played just for me. Looking back, maybe I should not have eaten the brownies. But both Jim Fixx and the Grateful Dead left deep impressions on me. Today I still enjoy both of them in some incarnation.

I look at my tattered Jim Fixx book and scan the shelves until I see his second book on running. Then I see my books by Dr. George Sheehan, the second running author I read, and I still follow Dr. Sheehan's advice. There is my autographed copy of John Parker's *Once a Runner* and Bill Bowerman's book on jogging. I see all the books that came out in the 1970s and 1980s that I missed because I did not see them in a bookstore. Of course, there was no Internet back then. There is James E. Shapiro's book on ultramarathoning and books by Arthur Lydiard. Over time, the trickle of running books turned into a strong current, which turned into a tsunami. Now, I cannot go to a bookstore without noticing another new book on running that will somehow find its way into the Mintzer home.

I have read most of them except those I use as a reference; thank you, Dr. Noakes. Reading them has ranged from a profound religious experience to an awful experience, but there are only a handful of books from which I have not learned something that made me a better runner. When I was a young lawyer, I had the opportunity to hear the great trial lawyer Gerry Spence. His advice to young lawyers was to try a lot of cases, and if you are not given that opportunity, then read books about trials. The same holds true for running. Running is a fundamentally simple activity that can be improved upon by practice, but it can be greatly enhanced by education.

So, why another running book? Because odds are I am writing from your perspective. I am a middle-of-the-pack—correction: back-of-the-pack—runner who in all probability has been doing this longer than you have. I am hardly an authority, but I have learned a lot about running over the last thirty-odd years.

Finally, I feel the need to do something about the poor shape of our citizenry. There is really no delicate way to say that we are becoming fatter and sicker. Exercise is not a cure-all, but it is one weapon in the arsenal to combat obesity and food-related illnesses.

Long ago, when I was obese, I realized that everything I thought was fun and looked forward to doing required the ability to move and some degree of physical activity. If I was blessed enough to have a relatively healthy body, I had better get it in shape since at that time my knees hurt with every step I took and I was winded after walking up a flight of stairs.

This is also a story about an unpopular fat kid with poor self-esteem who took up running, lost the weight, became moderately popular, slightly elevated his self-esteem, married above himself, had intelligent children, ran for his adult life, and completed a few marathons. So it is an inspirational story as well.

I hope that when you are looking at your running books several years from now, you will see mine, feel inspired, and remember something you learned from it (and did not think it was awful).

BOOK I

CHAPTER 1

As it turns out, my recollection of a series of events that occurred more than thirty years ago makes for a much better story than the actual things that transpired. Consequently, I will proceed to share with you the events as I remember them—and not as they happened.

I was in high school, and as families used to do in those days, my mother, stepfather, sister, and I were watching television in the living room. My sister and I completed our homework and sat down for dinner with Steve and my mother. If I was home for dinner, I must not have been working at my part-time job at Kentucky Fried Chicken. We were watching one of three major networks since cable or satellite had yet to enter the American lexicon as items being related to the television. The movie on television that evening was *See How She Runs* with Joanne Woodward. In the movie, Joanne Woodward overcomes a series of obstacles, calamities, and indignities before and during the Boston Marathon.

I found the movie particularly inspiring. If she could run a marathon, so could I. Despite watching the movie, I really did not have a very good grasp of how to train for a marathon, what type of gear I needed for a marathon, or where a marathon took place besides Boston; I could not even think of anyone I knew who had run a marathon. The Internet had yet to be invented, and the only place to get those questions answered would have been the library. Jim Fixx had yet to pen his classic tome on running. In retrospect, the library might not have been particularly enlightening either. This was the late 1970s; and I had neither had never heard of a running store nor set foot in a sporting goods store. Why would I?

That night, I set my alarm to awake early and went to bed. When my alarm went off, I got dressed and trudged to my high school track, which was conveniently located within walking distance from my house.

I wore a pair of blue suede Puma athletic shoes with a white stripe. They had slightly more support and padding than the box they came in. I was so proud of them. I worked the better part of three shifts at my fast-food job to be able to afford them. At that point, the only athletic clothes I owned happened to be the gym uniform that would have been stinking and mildewing in my gym locker another two hundred yards past the track.

Since the school was locked at that time, I had to improvise. I wore white tube socks with a ring of color just below my knees, a pair of cut-off Levis, a chambray shirt, and a jacket. I timed myself with my trusty Timex Dynabeat on the Twist-O-Flex bracelet my grandmother gave me.

On that cool, dark morning, I was training for my marathon. I started out slowly and managed to complete two and a half miles. I was so proud of myself for running around the track ten times. I knew that I could run a marathon; I could be like Joanne Woodward. I wanted so much to be like her at the end of the marathon, and I was on my way. I was going to do it.

I set my alarm to get up early the next morning and slept in. I continued that practice till the dreams of the marathon disappeared, and then I was able to set my alarm clock without a twinge of guilt.

Truth be told, it would be more than two years before I ran a step that was not at the request of a gym teacher—and thirty-two years before I felt like Joanne Woodward's character, finally finishing a marathon.

CHAPTER 2

My birth evidenced one of the few timed events where I actually beat the majority of the field at any timed event. The competitors were floating around in amniotic fluid for nine months, but I was out a good six weeks ahead of schedule. I was told that this was not a good thing. I was a very sick baby, spending the first weeks of my life in a hospital and then going back again after a short time at home.

Two years and nine months later, my sister followed. We lived in at least two houses and two apartments before we moved to a small ranch in St. Louis County. I live there through my first year of college. I started kindergarten after missing the first semester, and my parents divorced within the year. My father moved away, and I would only see him intermittently until my law school years.

At that point, I had not developed any athletic ability. I did not possess a baseball glove or football and had never watched a professional sporting event on television. In our rural area, neighbors were few. My sister and I played—but nothing that required fitness, coordination, or athletic skill.

The divorce brought to light a problem that was not resolved until I was away at college. My single mother did not drive. My sister and I were isolated except for the time we spent in school. We would walk about a third of a mile to the bus, go to school, come home on the bus, and walk the same rock road back to our house. We did not engage in afterschool activities or any social events because we had no way to get there or get home. We were fortunate to have horses; however, we did not start riding until we were older. With my father gone, my mother supported us by taking care of boarded horses. Since she was the only employee of her business and the horses required constant care, there was not a lot of time for frivolity.

When I was in third grade, my mother started dating. He was a microbiologist with two children, a boy my age and a girl slightly older than my sister. I did not get along with the boy particularly well, and I had a hard time adjusting to sharing my mother with another person. I had an even harder time being disciplined and taking orders from this interloper. As fortune would have it, they got married. At the time, I could not have perceived things getting worse, but they did.

In fourth grade, I had the first teacher who I absolutely detested and could not get along with. My new living arrangement at home and hating school were more than I could handle. For the first time in my life, I began making poor grades. There was even discussion of holding me back and having to repeat the grade.

At that point, I noticed something else. It was not enough that I lived in an area with no other kids. The invitations to the other children's parties and events quit coming after we had not responded to them in the preceding years. I felt like an idiot because I was failing fourth grade, and my lack of physical prowess guaranteed that I was the last person to be chosen for any athletic event in gym class or recess. To top matters off, I was becoming fat.

To me, it was not a gradual process. I just woke up one morning and realized I was fat. The association between eating and stress and unhappiness never registered with me. It also failed to register that the large amount of food I was eating was the cause of my newly discovered weight gain.

Unlike today, being heavy as a child was an oddity. Instead of having other heavy peers, I was it. When I was a heavy child, it was not mainstream or acceptable to be overweight. You could not buy your clothes in normal stores. The adult who took me shopping, usually my grandmother, had to take me to a store with a husky section. To add insult to injury, the manufacturers of husky clothes felt no need to make them stylish. I owned and wore two identical pairs of blue glen plaid pants because that was all my grandmother could find on that particular excursion to fit me. I dutifully wore them over and over. They were not back then—nor will they ever be—described by any junior high school student as cool.

Sometime in junior high school, my mother divorced her second husband. Whatever contact we had with the outside world was limited to school and whatever activities we would engage in with children who kept horses with my mother.

A police officer, Bill Zipf, kept a horse with us. He allowed me to follow him around at our stables and told me stories of his service in Vietnam and on the streets of St. Louis. I was intrigued. I will always be grateful for the time he spent with me. Up until I went away to college, he was my best friend and the only adult male figure in my life. I will never know what inspired him to dedicate so much time to such a peculiar child, but I will always be grateful to him.

Sometime around my fifteenth year, two notable things happened. A man my mother was seeing moved in, and I got my first job outside the stable. My mother's new boyfriend was younger than she was. He had never had any children of his own and was not sure how to handle us. If I struggle to remember some happy incident, I can. The overwhelming majority of my recollections focus on the fact that he was a tyrant and an abusive alcoholic. Before school, my sister and I would eat our cereal and milk or Campbell's chicken noodle soup, which my sister enjoyed—and he would be drinking his Ambassador Scotch and milk. I recall lots of screaming, yelling, crying, and getting hit. My most prevalent memories from the time were lying in bed listening to my mother and her boyfriend scream and things getting broken.

A high school-aged girl who kept a horse with my mother found a part-time job with Kentucky Fried Chicken. Even though the restaurant was a good mile and a half away, I applied. I was hired, pending my ability to get permission from my high school because of my age. The waiver was obtained, and off to work I went.

Anyone who has worked in the kitchen of a fast-food restaurant probably does not have very fond memories of the work. It is hard and dirty. However, despite the nature of the work, I thought I was in heaven. I was interacting with kids my age, and despite my ever-increasing girth, my fast-food peers accepted me as an equal. I learned about music, cars, and dating. I was even interacting with the opposite sex in a meaningful way for the first time in my life.

There was a downside I failed to realize at the time. As employees of Kentucky Fried Chicken, we were allowed to eat whatever we wanted with rare exception. Since we were never given breaks, we had to eat on our feet. I conditioned myself to eat a lot and eat it fast. Looking back, I am pained to think about the amount of fried chicken I would eat while running around the kitchen. I would ask for the leftover chicken, which I would carry home for my family, so I was eating it seven days a week at least two meals per day.

The other downside arose when you placed a group of high school kids in a kitchen with a little bit of money and at least one car between them. For the first time in my life, I was exposed to drinking and whatever trash-grade marijuana we could score. Beer, pot, great music, good company, and all the chicken I could eat, which tasted much better when I was high, really took the drudgery out of the kitchen work and the rest of my life. It was the bright spot in my life. This bliss lasted until my last high school summer ended and most of my friends and coworkers left for college. I quit my job, and because of my girth, I was hired as a bouncer in a game room. In retrospect, I question how menacing a fat, rosy-cheeked kid with particularly thick, oversized glasses could have been. I was grateful that our clientele was mostly kids—and the matter never had to be addressed.

After high school, I started the next fall at the University of Missouri St. Louis (UMSL). It never really occurred to me—or my family—that I could go away to college. It also never occurred to my parents, or me for that matter, that perhaps money should have been budgeted for my college education. Alternatively, maybe I should have sought some type of financial assistance. I cannot blame them since neither of my parents went to college, and I was not really concerned about my future.

My ability to attend college at all was made possible by three events. First, a high school counselor who had taken an interest in my welfare suggested I should sit for the ACT. Second, for reasons unknown, I applied to UMSL. The final event was throwing a keg party on graduation night at my house and charging two dollars a head for all the beer my classmates could drink; the success of this event addressed the financial aspect of attending a commuter college if I got a part-time job. I had everything under control for the first year.

Even though I liked many of my classmates, I hated UMSL. The daily commute was brutal, and it was even more punishing in inclement weather. I hated ten of my thirteen hours my first semester: pre-calculus and inorganic chemistry. When I failed pre-calculus and earned a C in chemistry, I flunked out of school. Fortunately, the college took me back on academic probation, and I managed to eke out a 2.75 average my second semester, which guaranteed my acceptance for my sophomore year.

In high school, my physical activity consisted of walking to school, gym class, and walking to work. During my first year of college, my physical activity was reduced to eating and the related collateral exercise such as walking to the refrigerator and standing in a fast food line.. The bright spot of my day was lunch, and all I had was a fast-food budget. Since the school was so close to the Illinois border, which had a younger drinking age, I was able to maintain my beer consumption. As one would expect, my girth increased. I remember labored breathing after any type of activity, mostly walking, and I had chronic bilateral knee pain. Of course, it never occurred to me that I was a physical wreck, especially for a teenager.

I kept in touch with my high school counselor. Gloria Eickmeyer. She never said so, but I am sure she was underwhelmed with my progress. However, she saw potential that seemed to escape everyone else. She suggested I get a fresh start by going away to college. That was welcome news since my alcoholic stepfather, a headhunter by trade, was trying to sell me to Captain D's as a management trainee. In his defense, I did have fast-food experience.

Since college sounded much better than a continuation of my restaurant years, I followed my counselor's advice. Also, for a year, I had been hearing stories about my friends' college experiences, which were much more exciting than mine. Mine consisted of academic failure and ingesting countless fast-food burgers with a six-pack waiting in my car. She suggested her alma mater, Arkansas State University, in Jonesboro, Arkansas. With loans, it was affordable. It was a four- or five-hour drive from home and small enough that I would not get lost in a large student body. I learned after my arrival that it was dry—but not as in lack of humidity. I could not purchase alcohol in the county where the school was located. I always wondered whether that factored in Ms. Eickmeyer's choice of schools for me.

So, like millions before me and millions after, I loaded up my Chevrolet, said good-bye to my family, friends, and coworkers, and drove south, hoping to conquer higher learning and make something of my life, which had been on the unremarkable side up to that point.

CHAPTER 3

From the back door of my childhood home to Arkansas State University was approximately 240 miles. It was the farthest I had ever driven by myself up to that point. With multiple stops to eat and ask for directions, I took almost six hours to get there. It took another two hours to find my dormitory, check in, and lug all my stuff from my car up to room.

Since my roommate had not arrived yet, I chose the bed next to the window. I do not remember how many days I was there before my roommate showed up. When Byron Wood arrived from Doniphan, Missouri, he was very friendly. We found out that we really did not have a lot in common. He was an outdoorsman, and one of his favorite activities was orienteering. From the way he talked, he was a very serious competitor and dedicated to the sport. On the other hand, I could take or leave the outdoors, and the only thing that really interested me was progressive rock music with an emphasis on the Grateful Dead. Until classes started, I could blare my stereo and pore over my two favorite magazines: *Rolling Stone* and *Relix*. Byron would go running.

Despite our differences, we developed a friendship. We started talking more, and then we started going to the cafeteria together since neither of us knew a soul at the school. We met more people and began to settle into college life. In one of our discussions, I let Byron know that I had been interested in running and had even thought about running a marathon. I left out the part that I only ran once and that the interest had passed.

Byron listened and was very supportive. He told me that if I just picked an afternoon, he would accompany me to a sporting goods store or a running store. The very next afternoon, he helped me pick out a good pair of running shoes. My first pair of running shoes was a blue pair of Nikes with a silver swoosh. Byron was a hard-core New Balance man, and even though Nike was not his preferred brand, he thought the shoes would do the trick.

I have read every book authored by John Bingham who is affectionately known as "The Penguin." John was twice my age when he started running and in much worse health; he smoked cigarettes and had more years to eat poorly and drink than I did. The Penguin vividly recalled every step he took when he started running. My recollection of similar events is not as clear; I ran around the campus. The course I eventually created was six miles; I knew it because I drove it off in my car. I ran to downtown Jonesboro and around the industrial plants, using my watch to crudely estimate my mileage.

I do not have any bad memories of when I first started running. In retrospect, this can be explained. When I first went away to college, my food portions were controlled by the cafeteria employees and my limited finances. As a result, my weight dropped drastically. I lost between twenty-five and thirty pounds during my first semester.

I had always been a forced walker. In elementary school, my sister and I had to walk to the bus in the morning and home in the afternoon. I walked to junior high and high school. When I started working, I had to walk to Kentucky Fried Chicken in heavy work boots and walk home if I could not beg a ride. When I worked in my mother's stable, I was either pushing a heavy wheelbarrow full of grain or horse manure. For a fat kid, I had strong legs. This coupled with my sudden weight loss and the fact that I was used to running slow (the only way I could run) enabled me to take to running with a minimal amount of misery and trauma. Up to that point, I had never done anything athletic. Because I had never pushed myself as an athlete, I stopped when something became difficult, unpleasant, or painful. Even though this is a despicable trait in a competitive athlete, it would protect a fledgling runner from injury. Oh yes, most importantly, I had just turned nineteen. Despite being heavy and an abysmal eater, compared to John Bingham, I was blessed with good health despite my artery-clogging, fast-food diet.

The first semester at Arkansas State had flown by, and my life was changing for the better. I was actually doing well in class. I was passing my college classes, and my lowest grade was a B. I had friends and was even dating on a regular basis. I had also fallen in love with running. I was getting stronger, faster, and thinner by the day. This was my first sustained athletic endeavor, and I was really enjoying it. Life was good, and my run was always the high point of my day. By my fourth month of running, I was easily doing six miles a day, and I felt comfortable enough with my accomplishments to call myself a runner. For the first time in my life, I was comfortable in my own skin and—dare I say it—thin.

I continued to run throughout my sophomore year. Running was the only physical activity in which I had ever participated where I could hold my own. When I ran with others, I could keep up. I was not dropping, missing, or never being given the ball. I was not being picked last or laughed at. I was running and keeping up with my peers. I could even run faster or farther than a few.

Since I did not have a summer job lined up, I decided to go to summer school. It would give me the chance to make up for the five hours of pre-calculus I failed my first semester and the paltry twelve hours I took my second. Summer school would increase the odds of graduating within four years—even though I had no concrete, long-term plans.

As far as this book goes, two notable things happened that summer. I entered my first race with several of my summer school running buddies. If my memory serves me well, it was a 5K (3.1 mile) Fourth of July Fun Run in Piggot, Arkansas. I do not remember my time, but I did not come in last. James Ferguson was an older student who ran with us. There were not any medals or shirts, but the winning runner, a fellow ASU student (Paul

Kassen), was given a yellowish-orange McDonald's T-shirt. Ferguson flew off the handle, and his hostility was directed at the race director. Pointing to us, his younger classmates, he sternly addressed the race director and made him aware that we ran as far as Paul Kassen did—and we should get shirts as well. The flustered race director left, came back, and gave us directions to a McDonald's in Paragould, Arkansas. By the end of the day, we had our shirts too. I still have marathon and ultramarathon medals hanging on the wall, but the pride I got receiving them will never quite match the pride I felt when I was given my McDonald's T-shirt.

The second notable event that occurred that summer was James Ferguson loaning me Jim Fixx's *The Complete Book of Running*. Reading that book was a life-changing event. I had been running for nine months, and I was totally ignorant of the sport. In fact, all I knew about running was I had hated it in gym class, and despite hellish adversity, Joanne Woodward finished her marathon. I learned so much, and I wanted to learn more. I have never enjoyed a running book as much, and even though I have gone back and read it again, I was never able to recreate the magic that occurred the first time I flipped through the pages of that book.

I ran throughout the summer, and by the time school stated in the fall, a regular group, including my dormitory manager (Steve Smith), was running my six-mile loop. My confidence increased, and so did my grade point average. Thanks to Byron's encouragement in my first semester at ASU, I ran all the way through college and managed to get my grades high enough to get accepted into a few law schools with a less-than-amazing LSAT score.

In retrospect, I wonder if I had a decent LSAT score at all. My friend Doug Farque and I enrolled for the Total Tape LSAT preparation class. In fact, we were the only two who enrolled for the class, and we were crammed into a room at the library that was barely twice the size of a phone booth, listening to the hypnotically dull tapes. Doug had to shake me a lot. We finished the course and went to take the LSAT at Memphis State together. We had the same dinner at TGI Friday's and shared a hotel room. We arrived early for the test and realized there were no pencil sharpeners in the building. This posed a problem since all we had with us were new, unsharpened pencils. I will always be grateful to the residents of the Pi Kappa Alpha house who opened their doors and magnanimously shared their sharpeners. We sat for the test in separate rooms. I thought I bombed it, and Doug felt good about his score.

We waited for our results. Doug was considering Ivy League schools, and I was finding the schools in the pre-law handbook with walk-on admission policies. Our results came on a Saturday. As luck would have it, the results arrived the same time as *Relix*, the Grateful Dead magazine. Since I had determined that my LSAT results would have nothing to do with my law school admission, I read the magazine first. When I was done, I tore open the results envelope and viewed my less than amazing 519. I could hear a few doors opening. Doug, on the other hand, scored an identical 519, and he heard doors slamming.

That summer, before law school, I got a job in Blytheville, Arkansas. I worked for an agency that provided services to troubled youth. I had an internship for the group my last year of college, spending my days attending juvenile court hearings and visiting my charges at summer school and home. I adjusted to the slow, small-town life in Blytheville. The highlight of my social life was drinking beer with a few fellow alumni at the Holiday Inn on Friday nights. Of course, the other highlight of my life was a daily six-mile run that would loop the whole town. I had company if someone drove over from Jonesboro to visit me, but my runs were a solitary pursuit. I do not remember seeing another runner the whole summer.

When I was not working, I spent my days listening to music and reading Jim Fixx's second book—and everything I could get my hands on by the late, great running doctor George Sheehan, Kurt Vonnegut, and John Irving.

In August 1981, I loaded up my battered Chevrolet Nova and headed for Houston to start law school.

CHAPTER 4

The drive to Houston took me one very long day. When I arrived, the town was dark. I met my father, and he took me to the apartment he had picked out for me. It would be my home for the next year. Less than a quarter of a mile from my apartment, there was a running path along Braes Bayou. A bayou in Houston does not really resemble a bayou in any usual sense of the word; instead, it is a very large concrete drainage ditch with running paths on both sides that go on for miles. I fell in love with those paths.

During my first semester of law school, a classmate—Van Gardner— introduced me to Memorial Park. Memorial Park was the crown jewel of places to run in Houston. The 2.9-mile natural surface path circled a large area of the park. It was estimated that 10,000 people a day used the trail. Runners and walkers used the park twenty-four hours a day. Anyone who ran in Memorial Park knew several routes that would lead to the Shepherd Drive/Allen Parkway/Memorial Drive Loop, which can easily add another seven miles to your run. The loop had paved paths and a parallel trail worn into the grass from years of runners hoping that a softer surface would reduce the chance of injury and allow them to coax a few more years out of their legs. The loop took me to the edge of downtown Houston, which was a wonderful place to run on a weekend morning because it was deserted.

Finally, I could take Fannin or Main toward the medical center, through the Museum District to Hermann Park, which is also a beautiful place to run. There was never a shortage of places for me to run in Houston. And run I did, at least three miles and as many as twelve miles a day, four to six days a week, weather permitting.

In my second semester of law school, I landed a clerkship. My excitement over employment in general, much less legal employment, was colored by the realization that my midmorning runs (all my classes were in the afternoon) became a thing of the past. For the first time in my life, not counting my single day of marathon training in high school, I had to get up in time to run and then get ready for work. Anyone who has ever made the adjustment from running any time but early morning to running only early morning knows what a difficult adjustment this is. It took my body more than a year to feel like five o'clock in the morning was a good time to run.

I ran through law school, the suicide of my mother's younger boyfriend, two more clerkships, an engagement, studying for the bar exam, my first attorney job, passing the bar, breaking the engagement, the death of Doug Farque by his own hand, my sister's marriage, my second law job, starting my own law practice, the birth of my sister's two daughters, the death of my beloved maternal grandmother, the estrangement from my father, a short failed marriage, one long-term cohabitation, three houses, four cats, two dogs, more jury trials than I can count, a great marriage, two children, four fun runs, and more than twenty years of practice before I ran the marathon I dreamed about in high school. Life certainly had its ups and down, but the consistent thread that held everything together for me was running.

CHAPTER 5

The racing bug never bit me. From 1981 until 2006—the year I ran my first marathon—I ran four races. During my second semester of law school, I ran a Law Day Run. In 1985, I attended the Association of Trial Lawyers of America's annual meeting in Chicago and ran a fun run there. In the late 1990s, I ran a race benefiting the Houston Museum of Fine Arts. I also ran the Rodeo Run where, upon completion, I got to meet Bill Rodgers, a rock star among runners.

In the summer of 2006, I was reading the newspaper and noticed an article about marathon training groups. After I read the article, it struck me that I was not getting any younger (closing in on forty-seven), and if I was going to run a marathon, I should do it sooner than later. I gave it some thought and told my wife (well, I asked my wife) that I was going to join a marathon group and finally live my dream—almost thirty years old—of running a marathon. Surprisingly, my wife agreed, and she stated that she wanted to run the marathon with me. This was even more amazing since she had given birth to our youngest daughter a year earlier. We were finally catching up on our sleep following Hayden's continuous colic, which plagued our family during the first five months of her life. By continuous, I do not mean a daily event, I mean screaming at the top of her lungs every waking hour.

Andrea and I sat down with the newspaper, studied the various groups, and picked one based on its size. With a smaller group, we thought we would get individual attention, and it would make our special event, completing the marathon, more personal.

When we began training for the marathon, I was not in my best running shape. I had let my mileage slip down to three miles a day, four days a week. In the previous three to four years, my eating habits changed from almost vegan to consuming almost anything I saw. In addition to being a little long in the tooth, I did not have much of a base—and I was carrying a few extra pounds. Running a marathon was going to be a major undertaking.

At our first meeting, we were given training schedules and went for a run around Memorial Park. I caught up with the founder of the group and was excited about talking to him about the sport I loved so much. I am borderline fanatical about purchasing and reading books on running. I assumed the founder of the group would be well versed and knowledgeable about running. About five minutes into the conversation, I realized this was not the case. To borrow a phrase from my wife, the dark clouds had started to roll in.

The next week, we ran a 5K fun run to determine what groups we were going to be in. My wife was in her second week of renewed running, and for the previous fifteen years, she had run slower than I did. We were put in separate groups, which defeated our plan to run the marathon together. Since I was in a group that was too fast for me, the obvious solution was to ask to be transferred to my wife's group.

From the very beginning, we had problems with the group. Namely, our group was the only one without a group leader. Therefore, nobody was there to lead our runs, and most importantly, we were never provided course maps like the other groups. I tried e-mailing the course director after he stopped showing up on a regular basis only to find later that he was deleting my e-mails. My wife and I took it upon ourselves to start creating our own courses, and that is what we would run.

My wife and I dutifully stuck to the running schedule. I had to get up earlier than Andrea did so I could run, get back to the house, and watch the children while she ran. On Saturdays, we hired a sitter to watch our children while we went to the group meetings and participated in the group runs. We had twenty-two weekends of sitters.

The marathon training was a bit overwhelming. On an eight-mile run, I ran out of fuel at mile seven. I struggled as I had never struggled to finish the last mile. In retrospect, I just ran out of energy. If I had kept a food log back then, I would have realized that I burned more calories than I consumed. I was too depleted to burn another two hundred calories. I was ignorant about it, and the first seed of the thoughts of failure became implanted. Of course, I tried contacting our founder—to no avail—and the seeds of doubt continued to grow.

To make matters worse, I developed increasing pain on the inside of my lower legs. I was in so much pain that I went to a doctor before our first race, a ten-mile aptly named 10 for Texas. So I could finish the race, the doctor gave me a series of at least ten injections in each leg. My wife and I finished the race, and for the first time since we entered the program, we were entertaining the possibility that we could actually finish a marathon. Following that, 10 for Texas became my favorite race. It was a personal milestone for us. Additionally, the course is flat, the race is run well, a large crowd turns out to cheer you on, and everyone parties at the end. Besides marking the first major positive event in my first marathon training, the race marked the beginning of running season for me.

Two weeks later, my wife and I ran our first half marathon. We completed it with a few walk breaks, but it was much harder than we thought it would be because of the "Houston hills." I call them Houston hills because they may not be recognized as hills in other parts of the country, but they were overwhelming to us. I did not realize it until later, but those hills I despised were miles twenty-four and twenty-five of the Houston Marathon. I would be seeing them in relatively short order—and feeling even worse. We finished the half marathon with respectable times. As buoyed as we were about this accomplishment, we were equally discouraged by our injuries and the complete lack of feedback from our group leader.

I believed that the solution to our injuries could be found in the shoe department of our local running store, and it was. Felix Lugo worked at the running store and had completed several marathons. He was also active in Houston's largest marathon training group, Houston Fit. I had known Felix for a while, and our friendship grew each time I went to the store and on the rare occasions where we would see each other while were out running. Besides being extremely knowledgeable about most aspects of running, Felix had a knack for inspiring and motivating runners. Felix's appearance was also very inspiring. Unless you saw him in motion, he did not look like a runner. He was average height and stocky. If he had been taller, I would have thought he worked the door at a club. Nobody would ever think of him as a runner. People looked at him and thought, *If he can run a marathon, so can I.*

On that Saturday afternoon, my wife and I shared our story of woe with Felix. We explained our injuries, our dissatisfaction with our training group, and our overall feeling of defeat and failure.

Felix's response was precisely what we needed. He assured us that even with six weeks to go, we had done the work. He told us that we had the miles and base under our belts, and even though long runs were ahead, we were basically good to go. Until the time that I put his advice to print, I never questioned whether his advice was solid, but it worked for us. He also gave us the name and number of a chiropractor who specialized in running and athletic injuries. We left the store feeling elated. Felix became our pro tem marathon coach. Every time we had a crisis of marathoning faith, we went to him. To his credit, he listened to us and answered all our questions. When we left him, we always felt better about our upcoming race. After Byron Wood, my college roommate who started me running, Felix Lugo became the second most influential runner in my life.

Scot Kelly was the chiropractor who Felix recommended. Dr. Kelly was a practitioner in a relatively new type of chiropractic treatment called Airrosti, which boasted rapid recovery times.

Andrea went to Dr. Kelly first, and despite the fact that the treatment was painful, she felt a little better. Dr. Kelly also provided us with a foam roller to use for stretching. I was still plagued with pains in my lower inside legs. Even with Dr. Kelly's aggressive treatment, I was slow to respond. I was a having a hard time maintaining my miles with the chronic pain.

Andrea was getting better, and I was getting worse. Dr. Kelly, in frustration, ordered an MRI of both legs. Even though some other issues came to light, none of them was major or debilitating. The MRI failed to indicate the source of my problems. As a last-ditch effort, Dr. Kelly asked that I bring him my shoes and run for him.

Dr. Kelly figured out the problem. Prior to the construction and use of my orthotics, I ran in a motion-control shoe, the type of shoe that has the most severe correction of a runner's gait. That was what worked for me without an orthotic. Since the orthotic also corrected my gait, the combination of the orthotic in a motion-control shoe overcorrected my gait, which was the problem. With Felix's help, I changed to a stability shoe, and with the constant treatment of Dr. Kelly, my injuries began to subside.

The morning of the long run finally arrived. Andrea and I were going to do our twenty-plus mile run. Since I was so paranoid about reinjuring myself, my desire was to run around Memorial Park seven or eight times. Andrea rightfully concluded that we would perish from repetitive-induced boredom. Instead, we started in the park and ventured out. Around mile twelve, I ran underneath a railroad trestle, and the ground was at a thirty-degree angle, dropping as it went from left to right. I felt a pain in my right knee. I ran another four miles, but I could not run on my knee any farther because it hurt too much. At mile sixteen, we had to stop running. We walked home, which was less than three miles away. When we got home, Andrea returned to finish her run, and I stayed home. I was depressed to realize the possibility of my running the marathon was nonexistent at that point.

I saw Dr. Kelly on Monday, and he started working on my knee, but it was not responding to his treatment. My personal physician prescribed me a steroid dosepak, hoping I would feel better in one week. I was feeling even more depressed since I had only one more week to run; after that, I had to start my taper. Finally, with the marathon less than two weeks away, I could run a slightly painful three miles with an apparatus on my knee. I told Andrea that if I could not run, she should run without me. She reluctantly agreed.

Literally days later, Andrea developed knee problems that did not respond to treatment by Dr. Kelly. My knee was feeling slightly better, and I was reconsidering running, but now it looked like she was out. Frantic, we called my physician, and even though he saw no point in running a marathon, he believed that if he examined her knee and did not detect any major damage, he could inject it so she could make it through the race. So, out of options, Andrea had her knee injected.

My mother-in-law came in from Dallas to watch our kids during the race. On the Saturday before the race, we consumed specific foods a friend had recommended. A turkey sandwich for lunch. Of course, I could not let all those French fries go to waste so I consumed a large quantity of those as well. For Dinner, we went to The Palm and had chicken parmesan. Concerned I was not getting enough carbs, I ordered another pasta and marinara sauce entrée. I was also eating the better part of the contents of the breadbasket. By the time I left the restaurant, I felt sick, fat, and bloated. I also had heartburn.

Earlier in the day, we went to the expo to pick up our numbers and look around. The expo was amazing, including shoe manufacturers, race representatives, and more running gear than you can imagine all under one roof. It is like a mini mall dedicated to running. Additionally, vendors give away all types of samples and trinkets, which our children were enjoying. I am a nervous eater. At that point, my stress level was elevated, and I was eating everything they were handing me. I consumed rice, rice and beans, energy bars, candy, and various hydrating drinks. By the time I left, I was feeling nauseous.

Following the expo, we thought it would be a good idea to drive the course. We started by the George R. Brown Convention Center and took off. I began to fixate that if we covered the course at that average speed of thirty miles per hour, we were going to be in the car at least an hour. By the time we got to mile six, which was less than a quarter of the course, I had myself worked up to a mild dither. Where Montrose and Allen Parkway meet and start to go uphill (by Houston standards), I was bordering on hysteria. The mileage we covered was insurmountable, and I could not take driving the course anymore. Much to my wife's disappointment, I terminated the drive.

By the time we got home, I had consumed so much food I thought I was going to give birth. I ran downstairs to the computer and looked at Weather.com for the seventy-fifth time in less than ten hours. I laid out my racing clothes and gear and went to bed. I checked the alarm at least thirty times and then thought of something else to fixate on. How do I run a marathon without sleeping the night before? I could not sleep. I was full to the point of being sick, had eaten myself into a sweat, and was unable to sleep. Andrea had gone right to sleep, and I watched the clock until three in the morning. I got less than two hours of sleep.

We got up, dressed, grabbed our wheat cinnamon raisin bagels, which we bought because they were so full of carbohydrates, and drove to the convention center. To appease my neurosis, we got there at least an hour earlier than we needed to. When we broke into our bagels, they were so hard they were inedible. I was afraid I was going to break a tooth. We managed to tear out the softer parts and eat those.

We stood around, and I am sure I was making the other runners nervous. When the runners started to walk toward the starting line, it hit me. I had to use the bathroom—and not in a good way. I am not a big fan of public restrooms in general. In the hierarchy of public restrooms, port-o-potties would be close to the bottom. But there I was, minutes before starting, having to use one. Andrea lovingly waited for me, and we continued toward the starting line.

Just as we were lining up with the five-hour runners, the Pledge of Allegiance started, and then the cannon went off. The runners began walking to the starting line and by the time they reached it, they were breaking into a run. When we crossed the starting line, the magnitude of our task struck me. I had six hours to complete 26.2 miles.

After we crossed the starting line, the magic of the event struck us. The crowds were lining the streets from the very start. When they began to thin out, I saw one of the most memorable sights of my life, which still amazes me every time I see it. I saw the sea of runners heading uphill on the viaduct—thousands of them—and they could not be packed any tighter. There was a pronounced bounce to them because they were running. The colors were the deep colors they get when the sun is not completely up. I simply love that image. One of the local networks shows that footage on a half-hour special that follows the late news on Houston Marathon Sunday, and I get choked up even watching it on the television.

After we finished the first mile, with 25.2 to go, we approached a working-class, predominantly Hispanic neighborhood. Even though it was early on a Sunday morning, residents, consisting mostly of families, lined the streets to cheer us on. I was truly touched, and their warm wishes catapulted us forward.

We proceeded west on Quitman to White Oak, and we passed the three-mile marker. Some of the magic evaporated on White Oak when we looked to our right, and a bridge abutment had become a makeshift urinal for about twenty-five runners. I tried to put that visual out of my mind and crossed mile four. We turned north in the Heights, and again, the streets were lined with people.

Right after mile five, we made a turn onto Studewood. At that turn, I got rid of my cotton gloves. Right after the mile six marker, we passed a sign for the Houston Conoco Rodeo Run, which taunted that if you were running the Rodeo Run, you would be done right now. At that moment, I vowed to myself that I would never run the Rodeo Run again, and I have kept my word.

Studemont crossed Washington and proceeded down to Allen Parkway at mile seven. Anyone who has run the Houston Marathon knows that is where you mutter your first profane word. By Houston standards, the next quarter of a mile is up a big hill. Of course, I was so pumped up that I went running up the hill, which seemed like a really good idea at the time. I would really rue that decision at mile eighteen. I was only running at one-third the speed of the course leader.

When I got to the top of the hill, the crowds were thick. Just past West Gray, I saw my first of two Luis's. My first friend named Luis had framed almost every piece of art Andrea and I own. I am sure I stated something really profound like, "We're running a marathon," and he wished us luck.

The crowds were heavy for the next two miles until the turnaround point for the half marathon. In short order, the crowds disappeared. In what seemed like a flash, Andrea and I were running by ourselves, a surreal feeling since the streets were so desolate; it almost felt as if we were in space.

As we ran by Palmer Episcopalian Church on Main Street past mile ten, we were sprinkled with holy water. At this point, it did not hurt to cover all our bases. We proceeded on Main Street and jogged right to run by Rice University. Tree-lined University Boulevard is one of the prettiest streets in Houston. It was less than fitting that we decided to stop at a row of outhouses. I exited the restroom, and with fifteen miles to go, my legs stiffened up. I felt as if I was running on stovepipes. This was a new and undesirable sensation.

I was trying to run with my stiff legs. After mile twelve, we entered West University. I ripped off my knee brace and threw it on the ground. This was not as bad as it sounds; everything that is thrown on the ground during the Houston Marathon is donated to charity. By this time, I had thrown off a rain jacket and gloves. With the brace gone, all I had left was my fanny pack, which was loaded with gels that I was ingesting at a frantic pace, fearing fuel depletion and a subsequent shutting down of my body.

The brace was one of many I bought while training for the race. Every time I felt a new pain, I bought a brace, lift, pad, or wrap. This was not money well spent, but I felt better after I made each purchase.

Somewhere between mile twelve and thirteen, a bystander offered me Tylenol or some other over-the-counter pain reliever. I swallowed the pills and kept going. My legs were starting to function again, and I was back in the race.

Right after the halfway mark, we turned right and headed north on Weslayan. On Weslayan, the crowds began to thin out again. The turnout on West University was large and inspiring. Right after we crossed Bissonnet, we saw our second Luis of the race. Luis Fabrega was a fellow lawyer and good friend. He was eating at Einstein's Bagels, yelled some encouraging words, and waved at us. His words really helped, and we pushed on past mile fourteen.

After mile fourteen, we made a left on Westpark and saw the largest hill on the course. I am confident that this would be recognized as a hill even outside of Houston. I was really feeling overwhelmed, but then I remembered being advised to walk the hills. Looking back as an experienced marathoner, I agree with this really sage advice. I should have taken it. For whatever reason, I thought we should at least run the majority of the hill, which we proceeded to do. After running as far as we could, we walked the rest. At the top of the hill, a marine in uniform was handing out red licorice. Thank goodness, I am a licorice person. I am sure that my crazed thank yous were unnerving to the young soldier.

After making a right on Newcastle, we made a left on the 59 feeder and headed toward Post Oak and the Galleria. Turning on to Richmond, we saw friends of Andrea's and pushed on. After that, I tossed my fanny pack. I had consumed all my gels but three, and they could easily fit into my running short pockets. We passed mile sixteen around the Galleria, and the crowds were getting heavy again, which helped distract us from the chore at hand.

We made a left on San Felipe, past mile seventeen, and made a right on Tanglewood. At that point, Andrea was ready to drop. Tanglewood had a large number of spectators, but I don't recall them as being particularly friendly. In retrospect, I wonder why all those people would be out on the streets on a Sunday morning if not to support the runners. They handed out oranges and water, and because it is a somewhat affluent neighborhood, they were passing out entire bottles of water. They were perfectly friendly, but at this point in the race, we were beginning to shut down. Everything was miserable, including us.

We passed mile eighteen and made a right on Chimney Rock, and then Andrea could not run anymore. We agreed to start running with regular walk breaks, although I was sure the walk breaks would cause my legs to stiffen due to the buildup of lactic acid (I visit this misconception later in the book). For the next three miles, we alternated between running and walking. After Chimney Rock, we made a right on Woodway, ran under the 610 loop, and finally entered Memorial Park with approximately six miles to go.

Things looked up at mile twenty-one. My mother-in-law was there with our two daughters. My older daughter, who was born to cheer, had made signs and began jumping up and down and yelling as we approached, our younger daughter was watching us from her stroller. Besides the girls looking very angelic, my mother-in-law came prepared with peanut butter and crackers and properly mixed red Gatorade. However, the real lifesaver at mile twenty-one was that our friends John and Jennifer jumped in to run with us for the last five miles. With almost an hour and a half to finish the race (barring a major disaster), we were going to be getting our finishers' medals.

We took off, feeling mildly refreshed, with our pacing team. It did not hurt that the remainder of Memorial Drive was lined with spectators. John and Jennifer did their best to keep us distracted with conversation while we ticked off the remaining miles. We exited Memorial Drive onto Shepherd and made a left onto Allen Parkway. At that point, approximately three and a half miles were left in the race. However, the next two and a half miles had several very oppressive hills. These same hills beat me up on the half marathon, and they were getting ready to finish me off. By the time I was halfway through Allen Parkway, running for thirty seconds nonstop was a superhuman effort.

Finally, at the end of Allen Parkway, right before we crossed under Highway 45, we passed the mile twenty-five sign. We had half an hour to go, and for the first time, I was sure we were going to finish under the six-hour cutoff.

At that point, we were walking more than running, but we pushed forward. We were slowly weaving our way to the finish line at the George R. Brown Convention Center. When the finish line was eight blocks away, we attempted to run, but we could not maintain much more than a walk. We decided to walk/run with the emphasis on walk until we got to the barriers that lined the street—and then we would run from there.

Right before the barriers, John and Jennifer left the course. We got to the barricades, which were almost three blocks out, but we could not maintain a run to the end. We took a few walk breaks until the last block, and then we gave it all we had. As we approached the finish line, my mother-in-law and daughters were yelling and screaming. As Andrea and I approached the finish line, we held hands and leaned in for a kiss. And then we were finished. Five hours and forty-two minutes after it started, we completed our marathon and would forever be marathoners. Almost thirty years after I first thought about running a marathon, I finally did it.

From that point forward, events become a little hazy. We entered the chute, passed former First Lady Barbara Bush, and got our medals. We walked over to get our finisher shirts and mugs. Since I am the crier in the family, I am sure that tears were rolling down my face throughout the whole process.

We walked past the barrier that separated the marathoners from the people waiting to receive them and found our family.

CHAPTER 6

There is really nothing anyone can tell you about how you will feel after a marathon that will convey the overall sensation accurately. Immediately following the race, we walked over to the host hotel and ate. We went home, showered, and napped. Following that, we ate dinner, watched a movie, and called it a night.

The next morning, I tried to get out of bed and could barely walk. My legs were stiff and sore. If I could actually move them, the pain would flare up. It was agonizing. I had to be in court the next morning, and I did not know how I was going to cover the three blocks from my car to the courthouse. I practiced walking, and even though it was painful, I could get around at a fraction of my usual pace.

I decided to take a few weeks off from running after a marathon. Andrea decided to take off a little more time than that—she decided that she would run again when hell froze over.

A few weeks went by, and the pain subsided in my legs, but it never went away. Andrea and I used those two weeks to catch up on our eating and drinking since we really could not drink much—if anything—before our runs, particularly the long runs. We went a little crazy.

On a cold February morning, I went to Memorial Park and attempted to run. When the pain in my legs was debilitating, I walked. I walked for two more weeks and tried running again. It was still painful and not fun.

I tried running without a Garmin or a watch, thinking a more relaxed run would put the fun back, but it did not help at all.

For the first time in my running life, I thought about giving it up. I felt that I had run my marathon but ruined myself in the process. I went to the bookstore and got a book on race-walking. That appeared to be a viable alternative.

I went around the house and tried to find my old bicycling gear. That crossed my mind as an alternative, but the solution to my running despair sat on Andrea's bed stand. It was *Marathon: You Can Do It!* by Olympian Jeff Galloway.

CHAPTER 7

Jeff Galloway has authored and published many books, and he is an incredible resource for running tips and advice. He has trained thousands of marathoners and has learned from them. He is one of running's greatest teachers and students of the sport.

The core principle of Jeff's running program is regular walk breaks. His highest run-to-walk ratio is a thirty-second walk break after completing one mile. His lowest run-to-walk ratio is five seconds of running followed by sixty seconds of walking. The average ratio is two to three minutes of running with a minute walk break. As it turns out, I have run at one time or the other using all of the ratios albeit the higher ratios improperly.

Prior to picking up his book, I believed that if I stopped or walked during a run, the lactic acid in my legs would cause them to stiffen, rendering me unable to run. I was so sure of this fact that I would stand and jog in place at traffic control devices or any other time I had to stop. If I saw a friend out running who tried to engage me in conversation, I would look at my watch, tap it, and run on. I have ingested pounds of crow since my first marathon; after all, Andrea suggested walk breaks during our marathon training and I put the kibosh on that perfectly rational suggestion with visions of lactic acid-induced paralysis.

I thumbed through the book and started taking walk breaks. Despite being a watch freak since grade school, I had absolutely no idea what an interval timer was. Because of this, I had to watch the time on my GPS and took thirty-second walk breaks after each mile. Amazingly, I was able to resume running after my first walk break and then again after my second. I sheepishly had to admit to myself—and Andrea—that I had been mistaken.

The benefit of the walk break is twofold. First, you get a break from the repetitive pounding of running and greatly reduce the chance of injury. Second, regular breaks will leave you less fatigued. The most amazing part of the walk breaks that no one believes until they adopt the program is that you will get faster over longer distances.

With my added walk breaks, running became bearable—and bearable transitioned into fun. The marathon did not destroy my ability or love of running. Just as I was getting back into the swing of things, I read that Jeff Galloway was going to be in town to kick off a membership drive for the local Galloway group. He was also going to be teaching a class afterward. I signed up for the class immediately.

The kickoff that preceded the class was held in a church basement. We were supposed to go on a short run with Jeff, eat breakfast, and then hear about the group and decide whether we wanted to join. Unfortunately, rain and lightning canceled the run.

While I was milling around the event, I met two women. Ila Owers and Carole Crittenden ran together in one of the Galloway subgroups that ran at a twelve-minute-per-mile pace, which seemed perfectly comfortable to me. They answered some preliminary questions, and I was hooked. They were stuck with me for the rest of the morning.

After the kickoff, the class started. My run intervals, which consisted of taking a thirty-second break after running one mile, was all wrong. It should have been around the three-minute run, one-minute walk break level. In six hours of class, I learned more practical things about running than I had in the previous twenty years. For the first time in my running life, everything came together.

CHAPTER 8

I began running with my new group. At the time, we were running for four minutes and walking for one. Even though the ratio was a little high for me, it was like heaven after my previous mile breaks (and prior to that, nonstop running).

Unlike my former group, Galloway was fully supported. There were fluids available before and after our runs as well as SAG vehicles for the longer runs. SAG is an acronym for support and gear. In our case, a vehicle would be at a designated spot with cold water, food, sports drinks, and on occasion, cold towels, which were a godsend in the Houston summer heat.

This time, marathon training was fun. Using the Galloway method, I did not have to see a doctor two times a week. I wasn't coming in from long runs so exhausted that I was spending the remainder of my Saturday sleeping the run off. I would come home, shower, and be ready for the rest of my day.

I will always feel bad about picking our first marathon group. It was such a bad experience that neither of us had a particularly good time, and I believe that it forever ruined the joy of running for Andrea.

We trained through the hot Texas summer, and before I knew it, fall and racing season were upon us. That last statement is only partially correct. Runners race year round in Houston, but the longer races are not until the fall when cooler weather sets in. No one wants to run a marathon or even a half when the mercury has passed one hundred degrees. Of course, runner desire is trumped by safety issues.

The kickoff race for me is the well-run 10 for Texas just north of Houston. I had talked the race up to other Galloway runners since I had enjoyed it so much the year before. Several of us participated, and the race did not disappoint. Once again, it was well run, supported by the community—including several cheerleaders along the course—and had a great party at the end with food, drinks, and entertainment for the participants.

The most amazing part of the race was that with the Galloway run-walk method, I beat my previous year's time. My next two races— the Houston Half Marathon and the 25K, both part of the Marathon Warm-Up Series—showed a marked improvement in my times.

CHAPTER 9

My next adventure can be directly attributed to a friend I met through my law practice. Layton Duer was a criminal defense lawyer who happened to be a very good runner. If you looked at Layton, the last thing you would think of would be running. He had played college football, and thirty years later, he still had the build of a football player. His arms were bigger than my thighs, and his chest was massive. Everything you read about the best runners weighing two pounds per inch of height did not apply to him; he blew that magic formula all to hell.

As I found out later, inside Layton's chest beat the heart of a great athlete. He was not affected by fatigue and pain like the rest of us. He was the kind of guy who ran the football forty yards for the winning touchdown with a broken leg. With Layton, you could throw in a compound fracture as well.

When Layton found out I was training for a marathon, he suggested that I run his favorite race. Sun Mart was a 50K (thirty-one mile) and fifty-mile race in Huntsville State Park in Huntsville, north of Houston. Layton was a fan of the race for many reasons. First, the race offered lots of prerace swag. Second, Layton told me that you spent the afternoon running in a beautiful state park. As he waxed on, he compared it to running a marathon in Memorial Park—without the monotony and with better scenery. He also said this race was so great that he did not run marathons anymore because they simply did not compare. With this image and his glowing endorsement, I signed up.

The day before the race, I went to the host hotel to pick up my packet. After I got my number and other race essentials, I was given a running bag. It was a rather large running bag—not the kind that would fit under your seat but maybe in the overhead bin. Next, I took the swag walk. The manned tables were loaded with goodies the sponsor was giving away. There were technical shirts, rain ponchos, sunglasses, gloves, timing chip fasteners, executive folders, caps, pens, and stuffed animals. By the time I was through the line, I was having a difficult time carrying my bag.

The next day, I showed up early for the race and visited the mobile kitchen feeding the runners. I met up with Layton and other Galloway runners, and we lined up to start. The fifty-mile runners left half an hour ahead of us. The gun went off, and Layton was off like a shot; he was a serious contender to win his age division. My group took off like a shot, but not nearly as fast, and we took regular walk breaks.

The first part of the race was on the road we had taken into the park. We had to backtrack just over a mile to the trail and complete two loops that were approximately fifteen miles apiece. We turned onto the trail, and I can only describe what resembled a scenario from an old World War II movie—a scene where the sniper is in the tower and people are just dropping. That is exactly what happened when the novice trail runners were introduced to roots. Layton never said anything about roots—or that I would have to watch every step I took for thirty of the thirty-one miles. This was a radical departure from my past running where I could count on the road or trail being level and free of hazards. You could think about other things besides your next step.

I soldiered through the first loop. Approximately every three miles, there was an aid station. Calling it an aid station was not really doing it justice. It was an ultramarathoner's buffet or a pot smoker's nirvana. It was stocked with peanut butter and jelly sandwiches, bananas, potatoes, pretzels, chips, jelly beans, red licorice, Oreos slathered in peanut butter, and any drink you could want. I became concerned about the real possibility of gaining weight during the longest race of my life.

One of the first things that struck me about ultra running as a middle-to-back-of-the-pack runner was the communal, laid back vibe. I can only compare it to the atmosphere at a Grateful Dead/Furthur concert—except you don't have to worry about getting dosed. If you were at the front of the pack like Scott Jurek or Ann Trason, life would be different, and you would be bothered by people like me you had to lap repeatedly.

The next thing I noticed was that I was smashing the hell out of my toes on all the roots. I was sure I was losing toenails, and I believed that I felt them in my socks. I asked Layton about purchasing trail shoes before the run, but he did not believe they were necessary.

When I felt my first toenail fall off and started to doubt this endeavor, I realized Layton was not human since he was undaunted by this race and kept coming back to run it again. The final thing we all noticed was that it was getting hotter than Hades. The thermometer read over eighty. You have to love Texas weather; in December, it could have been freezing or burning, and I was suffering through the latter. I later learned that a large percentage of the field dropped out because of the heat, but for whatever reason, nobody in my group ever thought about not finishing. Perhaps we were like the frogs in the gradually warming water and did not realize we were being cooked.

I finished the first lap, and I was two hundred yards from my next buffet on the final stretch. I took my eyes off the trail—and down I went. I am six foot two and hover around two hundred pounds, and I went down hard. Besides my ego, I checked for other damage. I noticed blood flowing from my left knee. I moved my leg back and forth, and everything felt close to normal. I got up and shuffled into the medical tent, which was located close to the buffet.

I sat down, and my knee started to stiffen. A nurse came over, rinsed it off, and asked me what I wanted to do. All I could think of was showing up to court and the verbal abuse I would be getting from Layton on Monday if I dropped out of the race. In particular, his pelting me with slang terms for female genitalia came to mind. I asked her to tape it up so I could finish the race. When my leg was wrapped, I asked about her training. She told me she was an accountant. On that note, I started my last lap. In retrospect, I probably should have had my knee stitched, instead, I have a permanent reminder of my first ultra.

The last lap was hard because of the heat. We were still making respectable time at 26.2 miles; we finished that distance in approximately six hours. However, we took over an hour and a half to do the last five miles, the heat reducing our running to a shuffle. At that point, we coined the term "SunMart shuffle," which has remained in my running group's lexicon long after SunMart gave up sponsoring the race and the very competent Roger Soler took over.

Approximately seven hours and forty minutes after we started the race, we crossed the finish line. Medals were placed around our necks, and we were given a choice of a blanket or a jacket. I picked the blanket, which remains one of the nicest finishing mementos I have received.

After I received my finisher items, I sat on the ground to take off my shoe. I knew I would pass out when I removed my shoe and saw the missing toenails. At least I would not have far to fall. I took off the shoe and looked. My toenails were fine, but there were a few rocks in my sock. I breathed a sigh of relief, rejoined my group, and went over to the mobile kitchen to eat and bask in our newly acquired status as ultra marathoners.

Sitting and eating, I knew I was never going to run this race again.

CHAPTER 10

The days following SunMart felt pretty good compared to my last marathon. I was subjecting myself to less repetitive pounding and actually giving my legs regular breaks with the Galloway method of running. Despite the root issues, trail running was even less stressful because your foot is not striking the ground the same way on every step. The surface on which you are you are running on differs to a certain degree every time you put your foot down. I could not run another marathon that week, but I could do an easy three or four miles.

I was approximately five weeks away from the Houston Marathon. Those in my group who ran SunMart decided that the race would be our long run. Since trail times are slower than road races, I was feeling very good about that year's marathon. I had seen Dr. Kelly before SunMart to go over everything and make sure my body was in working order. I saw him again the Friday before the Houston Marathon and felt I was as prepared as I was going to be.

My group met that morning, and with little time to waste, we were off and running. Well, running and regularly walking. My running group stayed together the entire marathon except for Susan Chang. At mile twenty-three, she decided she had spent enough time on the course (and probably with me) and took off.

As I ran the last blocks of the race, I saw my wife and children yelling and screaming (the third time that day I had seen them on the course). I picked it up as I crossed the finish line, taking thirty minutes off the previous year's time.

CHAPTER 11

For the next two years, my running calendar was identical. I ran at least four miles on Mondays, Wednesdays, and Thursdays. On Saturdays, I would go on a long run with my group. In the fall, I ran 10 for Texas, the Houston Half, the Houston Master Sports Association 25K, SunMart, and the Houston Marathon.

My view of trail running took a drastic change when I learned that the more you do it, the easier it becomes. My second SunMart was actually enjoyable, and I became a more efficient trail runner. Much to the disappointment of the worldwide running community, SunMart pulled its sponsorship. We thought the race was going to go away, but Roger Soler stepped up and continued to put on the same race—minus the swag and the mobile kitchen. Despite those losses, I was grateful since the race was the perfect long run before the Houston Marathon and great race on its own merit.

I was approaching fifty and thinking about Felix Lugo. He had turned fifty while I was preparing for my first marathon. To celebrate this special event, he ran the fifty-mile SunMart race, which was tough because of the distance and time constraints. The time restraints could be a factor for a middle-to-back-of the pack guy. Felix was a solid middle-of-the-pack guy. Much to his credit and dogged determination, Felix finished the race in time. This feat was an inspiration for me, and that is what I wanted to do to mark my fiftieth year.

When I brought this up to my wife, the idea did not go over very well. She had visions of a trip or a party—not standing in the middle of a park with the children for the better part of the day while watching her husband run himself into the ground. Finally, a compromise was reached: we would have a party around my actual birthday in September, and I would run the Rocky Raccoon fifty-miler the next February. It would still be my fiftieth year.

Besides being concerned about a fifty-miler in general, which is eighteen miles farther than I had ever run (one year, I went off course at Roger Soler's 50K and covered some extra real estate, bringing my total to just over thirty-two miles), it was two weeks after the Houston Marathon, which I was already registered for. To further compound the situation, Rocky Raccoon fell on the same date as my children's school's major fundraising gala. Short of running the best times in my life, somewhere in the world-class range, I would not be able to make the function. My wife concluded that she would have more fun volunteering with a friend at the fundraiser than attending it with me. All I had to do was complete the Houston Marathon without getting injured or contracting a post-marathon bug.

I had heard through the grapevine that my good friend Allen Lazenby was planning to run the same fifty-miler after the Houston Marathon as well. We started e-mailing each other back and forth and were getting very excited about the two races. We even bought new Garmins,(a GPS watch that measures your mileage and pace), because our current models held a charge for only eight hours. God forbid we should not be able to keep track of our miles and time on a fully supported and marked course.

Then what I took for disaster struck. Allen developed a sinus infection and could not run the Houston Marathon. I felt terrible for Allen, and then I selfishly began to think about myself. I had originally anticipated running the fifty miler by myself, and when I learned that Allen was going to run it, I set my sights on running the race with him. Now that he was under doctor's orders not to run Houston, I began to wonder about Rocky Raccoon, which was only two weeks away.

On the morning of the Houston Marathon, Allen looked good. He took not running the race very well—much better than I would have. With his best wishes, I ran the race, and the countdown to the fifty-miler began.

In hindsight, I did not prepare correctly. The day after the marathon, I took a long walk in an attempt to expedite function to my legs. By Wednesday, I was running my usual workout, which I kept up until the Thursday before the race. Surprisingly, my legs felt good. However, as I later learned, I should have rested them more.

On the morning of the race, I showered, foam rolled, dressed, and drove to Huntsville State Park. I brought enough gear in my bag since it was near freezing when we started and was to warm up considerably during the day.

Allen was a step ahead of me. He brought sufficient gear—and a tent, chairs, extra food, drinks and Becky, the head of another Galloway group who graciously functioned as crew chief and cheerleader. To support Allen and Becky, Allen's wife was also there. I would be remiss if I failed to mention that that Becky and Allen's wife were very accomplished runners in their own right.

I learned that another Galloway runner was going to be running the race as well. I had seen Bruce Evans before, but we had never been formally introduced. Bruce's next long race was going to be a fifty-miler or a 100K in California. Many ultra races had timed distance goals you need to meet or exceed to guarantee that you would finish the race before the cutoff time. For example, you might have a twelve-hour cutoff time to finish a fifty-mile race. If you have not completed at least forty miles by the ten-hour point, it was possible that you would be not allowed to participate in the race any further because you were not likely to finish the in the time allotted by the race organizers. Almost all marathons have a six to eight-hour cutoff before the course closes. It is a heartbreaking necessity of organizing races.

In order to stay in Bruce's next race, he needed to finish 50K (31 miles) in seven hours. That was faster than I had ever run 50K, and if I remember correctly, faster than Bruce had ever run that distance. We agreed to attempt to simulate the pace that Bruce would have to maintain in his next race.

The weather was cold when the race started. Ice had formed on the ground around the puddles—and there were a lot of puddles. Considering I had just run a marathon two weeks earlier, I felt pretty good. My first mistake caught up with me after the first few miles. Since it was a fully supported race, I did not bring any extra water or anything to carry it in. I assumed that the spaced water stops would be sufficient to keep me hydrated. After the first water stop, I was already suffering from thirst and dehydration issues. Allen, being the class act he is, gave me a seven-ounce hydration belt bottle. I immediately drained it, but at least I could drink more at the water and food stations and have something to help tide me over on the course.

With the water issue under control, I felt better about the race. I felt like an idiot for making such a stupid mistake. But, I was confident that I could still see the race through. The race was going well even at this breakneck pace—up until mile twenty-five or so. The abysmal water planning and personal-best pace caught up with me. I held back and let Allen and Bruce go on. My walk breaks were becoming longer, and I knew the next twenty-five miles were going to be rough.

I looked at my watch at mile thirty-one. I was only a few minutes off my targeted time. Of course, the other two guys were nowhere in sight. I pulled into our encampment two-thirds of the way through the race, feeling sorry for myself because I could not keep up with the other guys. I would have to complete the race by myself. I sat down to change socks and have my feet taken care of by Becky. She popped my blisters and put second skin over the punctures. I was good to go. I ate a little and sheepishly asked how the other guys were doing. I noticed that Bruce was still there. I had never been so happy to see anyone as I was to see Bruce.

As it turned out, Allen was feeling great since he was the only one with fresh legs. Bruce had just run a personal best on his 50k and had run the marathon, and he was feeling slightly better than I was. We grabbed our headlights and took off. I cannot think of a time when there was any less spring in my step. After a few miles, our speed slowed. Our walk breaks were getting longer, but we pushed on.

During the first two laps, Allen kept us entertained with stories from his life in the oil and gas business. We also uncomfortably realized that Allen and Bruce are pretty conservative guys, and I am pretty liberal. To further strain matters, Bruce is a policeman, and I am a criminal defense attorney. I am sure that Bruce initially viewed me as kind of a Karl Marx with horns and a tail or a beast with 666 tattooed somewhere on my body.

Very much to Bruce's credit, our differences were immediately set aside. During our last sixteen miles, we had wonderful conversations about family and all we had in common. As the run began to wind down, we were on our way to becoming good friends. Bruce also brought a piece of equipment that saved our lives in the dark: a flashlight. Despite having read numerous reviews on various head lamps and spending an evening talking to an REI employee, I had chosen a lamp that did not perform as well as I would have hoped. The path in front of me was not brightly illuminated. In fact, it was barely illuminated at all. Without Bruce's flashlight, our last lap would have been treacherous.

As we got closer to fifty miles, we began to pick up the pace. By the time we reached the last quarter mile, we were in a flat-out run. And then finally and suddenly, the distance, which hours before had seemed insurmountable, was covered. The three of us had completed the race.

Allen finished more than an hour before we did. He was showered, changed, and rested by the time we finished. As we started to walk around, I began to shake. Surprisingly, my legs were still functioning pretty well. Like my first SunMart, I swore I would never subject myself to that race again. After three years, I find myself looking at the registration form online. I know there is one more fifty-miler left in me.

And Why Even More on Running?

At this point in the book I have a pretty good idea of what you mightbe thinking. Do I really have to read more self-indulgent blather? Well, kind of. The self-indulgence will subside but not completely disappear and the focus will turn to my observations and information that I have learned in over thirty years of running. I hope that all of this will be interesting, helpful, and at least slightly amusing.

BOOK II

CHAPTER 12

When I first bean thinking of writing a book about running, my first thought was running shoes. In thousands of books and articles, you will be told that the only piece of equipment you need for running is a good pair of running shoes. Amusingly enough, at this time in running history, there is a movement in running—supported by the shoe manufacturers—for minimalist shoes for road and trail. This movement contends that the last piece of equipment you need is running shoes.

I have not joined the minimalist movement. It may have merit, but I have been running mostly injury free for the last several, Galloway-influenced years. Since my running is going well, I do not want to change anything. Sometimes when I am not running, I wear minimalist shoes because I believe the lack of cushioning and guidance will strengthen certain leg muscles, which will benefit my running.

When I decided to venture into the unknown world of running, my college roommate took me to a sporting goods store to buy proper running shoes. When those shoes developed a manufacturing defect, I exchanged them for another pair. The new pair was slightly cheaper and was made by another manufacturer. I remember Byron's disappointment at my choice because he pointed out the lack of support, flexibility and padding. I ran in those shoes, and Byron was absolutely right. I had made a mistake and corrected it as soon as I was financially able to.

When I first started running, all shoes were neutral. They provided very little support or cushioning. The shoe of my youth is a less technical version of today's minimalist shoe. The first running shoes I bought in 1978 were made of nylon and had the famous waffle bottom. I do not recall the model of those Nikes, but they were closely related to today's Pegasus. I loved them, and they felt better than anything I had ever put on my feet. I was amazed by how little they weighed.

Prior to those shoes, my athletic shoe choices had been dominated by Adidas and Puma. As far back as I can remember, gym shoes were made out of canvas. In sixth or seventh grade, I noticed other kids starting to wear red or blue suede athletic shoes with three white stripes. They were the coolest things I had ever seen. I found out that they were made by Adidas, which I could not pronounce, and that the particular model was called the Varsity. I found out where those beautiful shoes were sold and began to think that ownership was a possibility; however, my balloon was popped when I learned that they were $19.95 a pair.

I knew that my single mother was barely making ends meet, and all of our clothes were purchased once a year by my grandmother before school started. At that point, I received one pair of regular shoes and one pair of gym shoes to last me the whole year. Since my father was obligated to send thirty dollars per week for my support, I asked my mother to tap into those funds. I was flatly refused. I had very little concept of how much I cost to maintain and did not realize how insufficient the money was. I broached the subject with my grandmother with the same result.

In the following year, I saw what I believed to be a similar shoe at a local discount store, Grandpa Pigeons, for four dollars. They were white with five stripes. I dedicated my remaining days to doing whatever I had to do to earn the four dollars. After I earned the money, I finagled a ride to Grandpa's to get my shoes. The shoes were paired up in a large bin. I used my junior high expertise to pick out the pair I thought fit best.

My love for my new shoes exceeded their utility. They did not fit properly—coupled with the lack of flexibility in the synthetic material—and they gave me terrible blisters. Furthermore, they did not breathe. As a result, my feet were hot and wet with sweat. The shoes began to smell. In a matter of weeks, the luster had worn off my prize purchase, and I could not wear them anymore.

Weeks later, I was trailing around Bill Zipf, who boarded a horse at my mother's stable. I saw a pair of Adidas in his trunk. They were worn but still had plenty of life left in them. They were mustard color gazelles with black stripes. He gave them to me, and they instantly became my most prized possession. I never took them off. I wore them until my growing foot caused the back part of the shoe to separate from the front.

Following their demise, I succeeded in convincing my grandmother to buy me a pair of red Adidas Varsity. I can still see her sitting in the sporting goods store in her fur coat, stating that nobody would ever pay more than twenty dollars for a pair of gym shoes. That image goes through my mind every time I purchase a pair of running shoes, which are more than $150 with tax.

Until my first pair of Nikes, I wore Adidas or Pumas for all my borderline athletic endeavors. Everything was done in these shoes with nonexistent cushioning and padding. There was nothing about the shoes that even began to address my foot strike.

In 1979, I spent the summer in Houston and bought a pair of yellow Nike LDVs with a blue swoosh. By that time, I had been running for the better part of a year. They were my third or fourth pair of running shoes, and up until that point, they were my favorites. At the same time, I also began to read running magazines and realized a whole world of shoes was out there.

For the next twenty years or so, I bought all types of running shoes based on their styles or colors. Sometimes I had to settle for whatever shoes were in my size. I also bought shoes because of their gadgetry. Adidas once made a pair with a tool that could insert a bar in the heel. The density of the bar varied, and the firmer you wanted the heel, the denser the bar. I was also a big fan of the lightweight Nike Huarache. I fell prey to the Adidas webbing on the heel and another Adidas gadget, a gyroscope built into the heel that turned faster than a helicopter blade. This instrument would control how your foot struck for the perfect landing.

It was not until I began to suffer injuries while training for my first marathon that I realized the type of shoe I ran in was important. Perhaps the regular increase in mileage, my age, or the evolution of my running style caused my problems. As I later learned, most of these problems could be addressed and resolved depending on my shoes. For years, I had ignored the articles on the type of shoe you needed or the reviews of particular types of shoe.

If ever you watch a group of people run at one time, you will notice they each run differently. They range from being smooth and efficient to people like me. If I were a racehorse, I would have been euthanized. I believe the smooth and efficient people have fewer shoe issues, and I think most of their problems arise from overuse. The rest of us have biomechanical issues that can be addressed with shoes, orthotics, therapy, or exercises that target specific weaknesses. It took me more than twenty years of running and training for a marathon to realize I needed to address my biomechanical issues if I wanted to keep running at the same level.

I could have avoided the majority of my injuries throughout my years of running if I had taken the time to be fitted by someone who was knowledgeable about shoes—or if I had listened to the people who were fitting the shoes.

Shoes can be categorized in two ways. The first categorization is based on purpose. These include training shoes, racing flats, and trail shoes. There are other purpose shoes, such as walking and cross training, but they really do not apply to running. The purpose of the shoe is self-explanatory.

The shoe that will address the overwhelming majority of your needs is the training shoe. This is the shoe you run in every day. It is heavier and has more support and cushioning than the racing flat. Racing flats are seen in competitive running and usually in shorter distances. They are lighter and not for the biomechanically challenged. If you are calculating how much difference an ounce makes over 26.2 miles—or if a coach is doing this for you—you need a racing flat. If you are just hoping to finish the race and do not have a prayer of winning your age group, trainers will do the trick. Trail shoes are exactly what they sound like—they are for running off-road trails. Most models are heavy because they have protected/reinforced toes and lugs on the bottom for gripping. They usually offer some stability to support you on uneven terrain. If you are running on improved trails, you do not need them. If the trails are *au naturel*—and you could possibly smash your toes on a root—they are a bargain at twice the price.

Because of their weight, trail shoes are not an ideal training/everyday shoe. However, if you are going to be running a few trail runs in the next several months, wear your trail shoes once every two weeks for a regular run. When you hit the trail, you will be used to running in your trail shoes, and they will be broken in. My favorite trail shoe had rubbed blisters on the bottoms of my feet before I fixed the problem by experimenting with a new set of inserts. I am glad that the blisters did not manifest themselves on mile two of an ultramarathon with twenty-nine miles to go.

When you delve into the second method of categorization, things get more complicated and confusing. In an attempt to clarify this mess, think about your foot hitting the ground. When you run, your foot makes contact with the ground. Your leg and foot's response to that is called *pronation*. This response usually dictates what type of shoe you should be running in. Until the recent surge in minimalist shoes that emphasize natural motion, it was believed that if the foot's range of motion was not regulated or minimized, then you would experience stress and injury. The overwhelming majority of running shoes sold by those trained in the art of matching the runner with the best shoe will pick the shoe based on how the runner pronates.

Four types of pronation are recognized in the running shoe industry: severe overpronation, mild overpronation, neutral, and supination. Most runners exhibit some form of overpronation, and the majority of those exhibit mild pronation. Generally, a severe overpronator will wear a motion-control shoe, the mild overpronator will wear a stability shoe, and the neutral runner and the supinator will wear neutral shoes.

With the advent of mail order and Internet running shoe stores, runners have used a do-it-yourself method to determine what type of shoe they need by studying the arch. I have never had much luck in the few times I have attempted to perform it. I would never use it to buy a pair of running shoes but here it goes:

1. Pour water into a container that you can put your foot in.
2. Put your foot in the container to wet the bottom of your foot.
3. Step onto something that will leave an imprint of your foot.
4. Use your unskilled and untrained eye to determine whether you have a flat, medium, or high arch.
5. If you have a flat arch, pick a motion-control shoe. For a medium arch, choose a stability shoe. For a high arch, find a neutral shoe.

The two times I tried this, I was less than pleased with the results, but I am sure my lack of success is more a reflection of me than the test. I also believe you need to consider several other factors besides your arch type to determine the type of shoe you should be wearing, including your gait and weight.

When picking out a pair of running shoes, go to a qualified professional. Go to a store that specializes in running. It does not hurt to bring a worn pair of shoes—preferably running shoes—but any type may help. Wear something you can run in so the shoe professional can watch you run.

I really respect two shoe guys in Houston: Jim at Fleet Feet and Justin at Luke's Locker. Every fall, I make an appointment during a week when they are slow to see what shoe works best for me. Unfortunately, manufacturers tweak their models every year, and the updated version of last year's favorite may not be the ideal shoe for you. One of my favorites, a stability shoe morphed into a motion-control shoe while still being marketed as a stability shoe. Foolishly, I bought the newest version of the shoe without trying it on. After a few runs, I realized they were ripe for donation, a moderately expensive lesson.

Now that you have your pair of running shoes, you need a second pair, preferably another brand. I believe that regularly rotating shoes reduces the possibility of injury by varying the repetitive pounding on your legs and feet.

Finally, the worst news of all: running shoes are meant to be replaced every three hundred miles or so. I am fortunate because I feel a twinge in my knees when my shoes are wearing out. I know it is time for them to go. I look at my running log and usually discover that I have three hundred or more miles on them. Do not try to push the mileage in your shoes; you are asking for trouble that will manifest itself in an injury.

As I touched on before, last year's shoes may bear no resemblance to this year's model. Even with the same manufacturer, there is absolutely no consistency in sizing in running shoes. I have worn sizes 10.5–13 in running shoes and have consistently worn a size eleven men's dress shoe. It never fails that the perfect shoe for you is the ugliest pair on the shelf— and not the good-looking pair that caught your eye when you walked into the store or the beautiful pair you saw in your latest running magazine. Once again, size, fit, and look are some of the compelling reasons you need a trained person to help with your running shoes. And this does not touch on the most important reason: the wrong pair of shoes can ruin your running experience.

I am not against mail order or Internet shopping for purchasing shoes. If you find a pair of running shoes you like, I see no problem in purchasing a second or third pair online, especially if you can get them at a reduced price. However, I am a big advocate of supporting your local running store. All of them in Houston give back to the running community by sponsoring races and other activities. I try to go out of my way to support them. If you asked my wife, she would tell you I am supporting them too much.

CHAPTER 13

As running shoes have evolved, so has running apparel. In 1967, Bill Bowerman—arguably the greatest track coach who has ever lived and one of the founders of Nike—joined Oregon cardiologist W. E. Harris to publish a book on jogging. The photographs in the book show people running in all types of clothing; most of them bear little resemblance to what we would identify as running clothes today. The book states that the most common jogging outfits are sweatshirts, sweatpants, sweaters, and old trousers; Cotton long johns are recommended for winter.

When I first started running, I wore cotton and synthetic gym shorts, cotton T-shirts, and tube socks. Since the shorts were not lined, I would wear briefs or a jockstrap. The memory of my high school gym teacher telling me that I was risking a rupture if I was not properly supported was instilled in my mind. I knew that my failure to wear a jockstrap would cause blood to flow down my legs—followed by feet of bloody intestines—with my genitals lost somewhere in the carnage. When the weather got cold, I added a classic gray sweatshirt, sweatpants, gloves, and a knit cap.

The downside to my low-tech apparel was that it chafed me in the most unusual areas. During warm weather, the cotton shirt increased in weight because of the sweat. In cold weather, sweat soaked my clothes, and the chill was unbearable when the wind hit. In all weather, my socks would get soaked, and I would pray that they would not bunch up and cause blisters.

Of course, then there were jogging suits. At that point in my jogging career, the jogging suits worn by the American team in the 1972 Olympics were progressive relative to what was later stocked the shelves. Sometime in my college career, I received a gray velour Pierre Cardin jogging suit. I know I could not have jogged in the elastic-banded, wide-bottom pants, and I would have been too embarrassed to run in the jacket. Interestingly enough, during the first running boom, the term jogging suit did not describe a utilitarian piece of athletic apparel; it was very dated high fashion.

In the 1970s, my mother sent me a pair of lined nylon shorts for my birthday. They were that royal blue that was so popular in that era and made by Adidas. I thought they were the greatest invention since sliced bread. Here was a pair of shorts specifically made for running that addressed my support and looming rupture issue—and it came with a matching cotton shirt. I had my first running outfit!

My running wardrobe evolved as I purchased more of those wonderful lined shorts—either Adidas or Nike—T-shirts, and footies. After all, when I saw pictures of cool runners, they were not wearing tube socks. My sweats for cold weather remained. When it rained, I wore a nylon windbreaker.

The next breakthrough I remember was Gore-Tex. At the time, it was revolutionary. It was a synthetic fabric that was waterproof, windproof, and breathable. The problem with Gore-Tex available in the running community in the early 1980s was that it was expensive. I was never able to afford it on my law clerk wages. The good news is that other companies started making materials that shared some of the magical properties at more reasonable prices.

A few years later came the advent of running tights, which were very practical on colder days. The question arose whether you wore them over your shorts, under your shorts, or maybe with no shorts at all. Like all form-fitting items, they were not for everyone. Many of the patterns were less memorable than others. It was hard to believe, but not all running pants were tapered at the time. Running tights were progressive in that regard. For the record, I was an under-the-shorts guy.

The biggest breakthrough in running apparel was technical wicking fabric. This material actually removed the moisture your body produced by coming in contact with touch points in the fabric and spreading it to the outside of the fabric where it evaporated. At least, that is the scientific explanation on the Internet by Discover Trekking Outfitters. The short of it is the fabric pulled the moisture away from you and helped keep you dry. After the advent of technical fabric, every other type of material for running apparel became passé.

Everything for the runner now is wicks moisture: shirts, singlets, shorts, socks, and jackets. The technical material is also made of lighter fabrics. However, as technology improved, shirts that looked like the cotton T-shirts of yesteryear wicked moisture as well. Additionally, as other technologies improved, there was lightweight material that was waterproof, blocked the wind, and kept out the cold. The days of running bundled up like a snowman are gone. Depending on the manufacturer, these items are reasonably priced and will last for years if you take care of them.

Shopping for running apparel can be a little tricky. Like shoes, there is absolutely no consistency in sizing. Sizing varies in different items from the same manufacturer. Be careful that the apparel you buy actually has wicking capability. Many items that look like they are made of technical fabric simply are not. Look for a tag on the garment or some type of mark that identifies its capabilities. I have purchased a few items that fit this description and can feel the difference after the first run. These faux wicking items are most common in outlets and discount sporting goods stores. You need not go broke buying the authentic items. Some of my favorite technical shirts are from a national discount store, and they cost one-third of the shirts manufactured by the major running shoe companies.

A recognized complication of the technical fabric is that after many outings, it begins to smell—and the smell becomes affixed to the clothes. I have read many reasons for this unpleasant phenomenon, and the majority of them blame the problem on improper care and bacteria. Improper care is not washing the garment regularly or in a timely manner. Also, for whatever reason, fabric softener acts like kryptonite if used on technical wicking fabric. If you have a compulsion to use softener on your running clothes, you might as well go back to the cotton T-shirts.

You might try one of the many specialized detergents designed for running clothes to keep them free of odors. I have used them before and the results were outstanding. However, I have received the same result by using Dreft or any other detergent for infants that does not contain softener.

I will end this chapter with a bizarre observation. I will preface it by expressing my love for REI. I spend the hours I am not working or running in a pair of their long shorts and a black Sahara T-shirt. I love Under Armour because their technical shirts do not snag—even if their fitted shirts cling to me like a sausage casing and accentuate every physical flaw I have, especially those that arise from the accumulation of fat.

But when I use glide, which I will detail later in this book, it stains their fabric—and only their fabric. One time, I threw on an Under Armour shirt in the early morning and went to the gym. While I was doing my unique version of curls, I looked in the mirror—and the shirt was stained. I could have lived with the stain, but this particular stain looked as if I was lactating, which was just too much for me.

I have had the same problems with REI shirts and cannot get the spots out. Now these shirts are relegated to being worn under others in cooler weather, or I put them on when I want to horrify my children in front of their friends. I'm still contemplating other occasions when I could make that perfect impression as the lactating man.

CHAPTER 14

I love watches. I have loved watches ever since I was a little kid, and I have not yet outgrown my passion. Believe it or not, there was a day when there was no such thing as a running watch. Well, there was a running watch, but it was your regular analog wristwatch you put on when you went running. Doubling as a running watch was your car or house clock that you looked at when your run started and then again when your run ended.

Prior to the 1970s, your watch was either automatic or wound by hand. After that, it was quartz. Then there was the advent of digital watches. Let us not forget the red crystal LED,(light-emitting diodes), watches and LCD, (liquid crystal display), watches which were not originally suited for running.

In 1986, Timex released the Ironman, which became the bestselling watch in the world. It changed everything. In all fairness to Timex, the Marathon and Triathlon models prior to the Ironman basically had the same features, but no other watch left its mark—and continues to leave its mark—on running like the Timex Ironman.

The original Ironman was LCD, black with orange trim. The case was plastic. The strap was rubber, which made it light, and it was water resistant to one hundred meters. It had functions that runners loved: timers and a built-in stopwatch. The buttons were big so they were easy to use when you ran, and it had a light feature so you could see your running time or tell the time when you were running in the dark. Who cared that it was a little difficult to set and the light was a little underwhelming until the advent of Indiglo in 1992?

Besides being utilitarian, the Timex Ironman identified you as a runner. It was the next best thing to having an "R" branded on your forehead. Despite the proliferation of automatic watches and the poo-pooing of the practice in fashion magazines and columns, you can still see the humble Ironman sticking out from under the cuff of some very nice suits.

Many running shoe manufacturers, including Nike and New Balance, jumped into the running watch business, but for some reason, they have discontinued their timely pursuit. The Timex Ironman keeps going. Dozens of different models have been produced, but for the most part, the features have remained the same. Not all Ironmen have my favorite feature, the interval timer, but it is available on several models. The original Ironman later became available with blue and red trim, and different models began to sport various colors. The greatest improvement of all is that the watch has become much easier to set and operate. As an additional bonus, for the aging runner, Timex has mercifully doubled the size of the numerals.

Runners have different opinions on almost every aspect of running. However, with timing, the overwhelming majority agrees on one thing: the Timex Ironman is the superior running watch of choice.

CHAPTER 15

L ooking at changes in the last three decades of running, perhaps the biggest breakthrough has been in the area of hydration. Dehydration is what occurs when you lose fluids. This primarily decreases your electrolytes and blood volume. The net result is muscle cramps, dizziness, muscle weakness, and the very unpleasant possibility of heat-related illnesses. I have been very fortunate that the worst thing that ever happened to me in a long run was the gradual inability to run because my legs had turned to lead. This was later diagnosed as an electrolyte imbalance caused by dehydration.

Runners can consume a number of types of drinks before, during, and after their runs. You will need to experiment with what drink works best for you. Because Houston can get so hot and humid in the summer, I drink fluids during the run—and I mix up a drink with an electrolyte-enhanced sport drink tab the night before any run over ten miles.

When I first started running, the choice of fluid replacement drinks was limited to water, soda, flat soda, and yellow Gatorade. Although these fluid replacements will do the trick on most occasions, today's runner has many more choices in the variety and quality of hydration drinks.

In 1978, when I first started to think about how to quench my thirst on a run, bottled water as we know it did not exist. In addition, there was nothing for a runner to carry fluids in. Looking back, I find this hard to believe because the bicycle I owned in high school before I even thought about running a step had a rack and water bottle that cleverly fit inside in cage in the event that I became parched on my ride. When I first started running, if I wanted fluids, I would leave a bottle in a bush, which was considered pretty high tech at the time. I could plan my run around a few drinking fountains or run around a track with a fountain or with my bottle on the ground.

Now, when you go into a running store or click on a running store website, entire sections are devoted to various devices to keep you hydrated. Basically you can choose from one of three types of hydration devices: the handheld bottle with a grip into which you can slide your hand, the fuel belt that goes around your waist and has bottles attached, and the CamelBak, which resembles a backpack with a bladder inside that you drain through a mouthpiece.

I personally prefer the large handheld twenty-two-ounce bottle. I tried the fuel belt, and the constant sloshing sound coupled with my inability to return the individual bottles to the pouch drove me insane. If I had to turn around to pick up one more dropped bottle, my head would have popped off. However, the majority of people I have run with love them. I have seen backpacks that hold up to one hundred ounces of water. I have never used one, but if I was to run a longer unsupported race, I would become very familiar with my favorite model. They do slosh, but the good news is there is nothing to regularly drop.

Staying hydrated requires serious planning, particularly during summer in warmer states. First, in the summer, try to run early. I usually try to start my run by 4:30 a.m. when it is a few degrees cooler, and the sun is not beating down on me. Plan your water. If you do not have a SAG vehicle waiting for you, know where every water fountain, coffee shop, grocery store, and convenience store are located so you can rehydrate on the way. Since I tend to drip all over the floor of establishments when I refill my bottle or get a drink, I always leave a dollar or two as a tip so they might be happy the next time they see a runner.

In Houston, particularly in August, all the running groups start marathon training. They all have water stations. I have seen stations turn away runners who have requested drinks because they were not members of that particular group.

To all running groups, bring a little extra water when it is hot—and do not turn a thirsty runner away. Yes, the runner should have planned better, but it is not a crime that is worthy of a death sentence.

CHAPTER 16

Put yourself in my position: It is 1977. You just finished reading Jim Fixx's *The Complete Book of Running,* and you want to learn more about this wonderful new (to you) activity. In the bibliography, Fixx refers to more than 225 authors and well over 300 publications, some of them as authoritative as a letter to the editor. Not even twenty of his resources are books, and less than half of those books pertain to running. Your thirst for running knowledge is not going to be quenched unless you have access to a fairly impressive microfiche collection.

Another great breakthrough in the last thirty years is the amount of information available on running. There are so many books on the subject that you could not read them all in a lifetime (I know; I am trying). There are several magazines besides *Runners World* and *Running Times*, and there are several lifetimes of information available on the Internet. Additionally, there are dozens of videos, from documentary, educational, or fictional/non-fictional dramas to major films about running and runners. Even my running mentor and coach Jeff Galloway has a video on running I have watched numerous times.

You cannot train for your first marathon without watching *Spirit of the Marathon*. The movie does an outstanding job of documenting preparation for the marathon, and it follows runners training from all levels—from beginners to professionals.

I have never read a book on running, even those that I did not particularly like or agree with, where I did not learn something or at least reexamine how I was doing things. My favorite books inspire me to run better, harder, and farther.

Running magazines are an incredible resource. They are full of training advice for runners of all levels and cover all aspects of running. They are also the first to bring you the newest shoes and technology-related breakthroughs. They are useful for bringing new books, films, and videos to your attention. I find their training and nutrition hints very helpful. I once sprained my ankle by falling into a flowerbed (don't ask!), and the *Runners World* that arrived later that week had the perfect cure for my injury, which was standing on the injured leg for regular intervals of time. It worked like a charm, and my downtime was minimal.

There is nothing more inspiring than the story of another runner. Whether the runner is a world-class athlete or the last person to cross the finish line in a local 5K, each has a unique story. Those stories have proven to be a great inspiration for me and keep me looking forward to my next run.

One of my favorite periodicals is *Marathon & Beyond,* which takes submissions from amateur and professional writers. There are articles about training, running history, recollections of races, and stories about famous runners. It is published every two months, and it is bound like a paperback book. When it arrives, it is a treat that I savor. The articles have practical advice and will keep you looking forward to your next run as well.

Finally, the Internet has more information about running than you could possibly absorb. I rely upon the Internet for product reviews, particularly about shoes. For classifying shoes, I am particularly fond of www.roadrunnersports.com, which has dozens of reviews for each particular shoe. Its shoe groupings are fairly accurate for finding specific shoes that will work for me.

The Internet is also a great starting point for the diagnosis and the treatment of injuries. Thanks to the Internet, I can read about runners who may not have earned their own biographies or their biographies are no longer in print. Alibris is helpful on finding those harder-to-get books, including anything written about running by James E. Shapiro.

Finally, on YouTube, you can watch great runners in their heydays.

CHAPTER 17

O ther changes have occurred in running in the last thirty-four years; they do not deserve their own chapters, but they are certainly worthy of mention. Please note that these are not listed in any particular order, but they have each contributed to running by making the activity easier or safer.

Dedicated Running Trails

When I first started running, I had three places to run: the road, the side of the road, and the track. During the first running boom, drivers were hostile and would think nothing of running you off the road, throwing things at you, or splashing you if given the chance.

And nothing screams monotony more than a nice long run on the track—no matter how wonderful the surface. Now, all over the country, runners and walkers have access to finished dedicated trails and paths. They are safe from hazards and are usually free of automobiles and other wheeled modes of transportation.

Local Running Publications

If a publication existed in northeast Arkansas in 1978 that listed all the running groups, races, and activities, I was unable to find it. Now, dozens of local publications that put this information at your fingertips are available for little or no cost. If such a magazine does not exist in your area, many running group and clubs publish this information on their websites so you will know everything going on in your running community.

Specialized Running Stores with Trained Personnel

I touched on this earlier, but I cannot emphasize enough the importance of trained personnel. When I first moved to Houston, the fourth largest city in the United States, there were two running stores. Some of their employees were very knowledgeable, and some were not. Nothing can ruin a beginning runner's experience more than being paired up with the wrong equipment, and conversely, nothing can enhance your running more than having the right equipment. These experts can enrich your experiences.

Running Groups

The last thirty-four years have seen a proliferation of running groups. I have seen running groups based on age, sex, political causes, charitable causes, recovery from addictions, and any other reason you can think of. Look on the Internet or in your local running publication for a group that is a good fit for you. Running can be a social activity, and with very little effort, your group can be your social life. And running with a group can be fun. It will certainly make your next twenty-mile run easier.

Training Groups

Training groups are usually not social in nature, but they have specific goals in mind, such as helping you get through a 10K or a marathon. I will be the first to admit that I was incapable of pulling things together on my own to get through my first marathon. As abysmal as the experience was in my first marathon group, the structured training was very helpful.

Even though a large training group may not be able to give you individual attention, it should be able to guide you to the specific resource you need to address every problem that arises. These groups have done a spectacular job of getting a record number of people across the finish lines of marathons. I wish they would focus on keeping more of their participants running year round instead of hanging up their training shoes after getting their finisher medals.

Glide

When I was in first grade, my grandmother sent me to school with a briefcase, and because I had chapped lips, my mother put in a tub of Vaseline. I am confident that I was the only child at Claymont Elementary School who brought those two items to school. Both items made me the instant object of the other kids' scorn, abuse, and disdain.

Following that childhood trauma, I avoided Vaseline until I started running and realized it was the only substance I could use to avoid chafing on my chest and inner thighs. It was messy, cumbersome, and difficult to wash out of my clothes. Then came Glide, the self-described original anti-chafe balm. It comes in a stick like deodorant, and with rare exception, it washes right out your running clothes. Need I say more?

Treadmills

Even though I have logged thousands of miles on treadmills, I prefer running outside. However, for thousands of people, because of travel, weather, childcare, safety, and a number of other reasons, the treadmill is the only way to run. The first treadmill I saw did not have a motor, but they have come a long way, particularly in the area of running surfaces.

I know runners who have been relegated to training for marathons on a treadmill. Even though this type of training was not their first choice, it worked for them.

Portable Music

I saw my first Sony Walkman during my last year in law school. I was running with someone regularly who put earphones on when we ran, thus ending our conversations forever. I bought one myself and ran with it for years. I would put a lot of work into creating cassettes so I would have upbeat, inspiring music the whole run.

I noticed three things happened: I was not doing my hearing any favors, I had a few close calls with cars, and I could not run without music. It took me a while, but I finally weaned myself from this habit. Music can now be transported in an item slightly bigger than a postage stamp.

While I am no longer a fan of running with music, I believe that if it gets you out there and helps you through your run, then go ahead. Listening to music while running is better than sitting on the couch. However, please be aware, many marathons do not allow runners to use portable stereos on their courses.

GPS

When I first started running and wanted to know how far I had run, I would drive it off with my car. Alternatively, I could take my total running time and divide it by my average pace. Before GPS, foot and arm pods would attempt to link with a satellite to get your time and distance. To say that they functioned erratically would be polite.

Within the past ten years, Garmin has perfected the technology for runners. Timex, Suunto and Soleus make outstanding products and are gaining on Garmin. Now, there is a wrist instrument that can give you accurate speed and distance. They are reasonably priced (around one hundred dollars with basic features up to five hundred dollars with many more features, including a virtual training partner). I use one regularly to keep track of my mileage and to help develop new routes. Obviously, with the use of GPS, everyone's training logs are incredibly accurate.

Racing

During the first race I ran in Piggott, Arkansas, a man with a stopwatch called out our times after we crossed the finish line. Some harried person would try to write down our numbers and times. Races have evolved to the point where racing chips are tied into our shoelaces or sensors in our racing numbers start recording our times when we cross the starting line and stop when we cross the finish line.

Timing, for the most part, is accurate and foolproof. I have also seen races turn into events with photographers and hydration on the course. A short race could provide food and entertainment at the end. Today's racer receives more than a timed safe course.

Eating on the Run

Once upon a time, there were no goos or other types of high-energy carbohydrate-packed portable nutrition for runners to take with them on their runs. Because of the heat put off by the runner (and not even considering the summer months), you would carry hard candy in a plastic bag (to keep it from melting) for an energy source on the run. Today, the choices are overwhelming.

The Foam Roller

The "stretch and don't stretch" debate has been going on for as long as I can remember. However, I have never heard anyone talk poorly or have a runner shy away from using a foam roller. Foam rollers have proven to be quite helpful for stretching all types of muscles without the risk of injury that can accompany a poorly executed stretch.

If you are not familiar with this item, Google "foam roller and running" immediately. Using the foam roller has become an essential part of my pre-run ritual and has been helpful in preventing injuries.

Advances in Traditional and Non-Traditional Injury Treatment

Even though he has done everything he can to keep me running, my personal physician had been predicting the destruction of my knees for the past twenty-five years. I am glad to report that his prediction has been wrong, and only one of my running injuries in the last thirty-four years has had to do with my knees. Sam Siegler is an excellent doctor, but he fails to see the physical or emotional benefits of running. Sam is in the majority of physicians.

Over the past thirty years, a group of medical doctors, chiropractors, and alternative providers has kept nonprofessional athletes active at their highest possible levels of participation. Over the years, I have sought and obtained relief from podiatrists, acupuncturists, chiropractors, and medical doctors. All of them have been dedicated to keeping me running—thank goodness that all of them have been successful in their efforts.

CHAPTER 18

This chapter deals with a subject that transcends running: nutrition. The late physical fitness icon Jack LaLanne believed that exercise is king, and nutrition is queen. Put them together, and you have a kingdom.

Unfortunately, as we scan the landscape, kingdoms are rare. Obesity, diabetes, heart disease, and cancer are on the rise. Two other disturbing occurrences are the increasing number of obese children and the medical community's belief that this generation of children will be the first to not live as long as their parents. What we put in our mouths—accompanied with our sedentary lifestyle—can have disastrous results. All you need to do is look around to see the carnage. Joe Cross, the juicing guru, said, "We are fat, sick, and nearly dead."

It was once thought that if you were healthy enough to run a marathon, then you would be immune from heart disease. Sadly, James Fixx, an accomplished marathoner, who contributed so much to the first running boom and wrote what many people consider the bible of running, proved that wrong on July 20, 1984, when he suffered a fatal heart attack on a run. The autopsy showed severe arterial blockage. Unfortunately for Jim Fixx and others, exercise and fitness alone are not enough to guarantee good health and longevity.

Exercise is helpful in combatting current health problems, but diet is as important—if not *more* important. Animal-based, processed food diets are killing us. We are among the sickest civilized countries in the world, and what we are doing is not working.

The solution is simple, but it is a radical departure from what we are used to: a plant-based diet. The facts are undisputed. In *Prevent and Reverse Heart Disease*, Dr. Caldwell Esselstyn shows a plant-based diet can reverse arthrosclerosis and other diseases.

T. Colin Campbell, PhD, the author of *The China Study*, documented the link between the consumption of animal protein and cancer, heart disease, and other illnesses.

Dr. John McDougall, another advocate of a plant-based diet, has documented positive results combating diabetes, heart-related diseases, and cancer with diet.

In *Skinny Bastard* by Rory Freedman and Kim Barnouin, our current diet and the food industry is laid out for all to see in a very colorful (well, profane) and rapid-fire manner. The book is concise and covers many of the reasons to support a plant-based lifestyle. By changing our diets, we are combating the causes of the disease instead of fighting the symptoms with surgery and medication. It does not make sense to take Lipitor so we can continue to ingest meat and dairy, which caused the conditions that required the statin drug in the first place. It makes even less sense to have your chest cracked open and your arterial blockage cleared out just to continue eating the same old way.

It is commonly believed that a plant-based diet will not provide us with enough energy to make it through the day, much less to exercise vigorously. The website www.greatveganathletes.com dispels that rumor. The great ultramarathoner Scott Jurek is a vegan. His accomplishments are too numerous to mention, but one is the twenty-four-hour run record of 165.7 miles. He candidly admits in his biography *Eat and Run* that a plant-based diet improved his performance and recovery. On the other end of the spectrum, Carl Lewis, a world-class sprinter, credits his greatest results to a vegan diet. In June 2012, Arian Foster of the Houston Texans came out as the first vegan in the NFL. I hope these examples demonstrate that you can thrive on a plant-based diet without beef, pork, poultry, fish, or dairy. Even better, removing those items from your diet will decrease the odds of contracting the diseases that now run rampant in society.

Let's address the misconceptions about a plant-based diet—namely that the food tastes terrible and that a plant-based diet is difficult to follow. Neither one of these is true; you just need to be creative. My wife has made wonderful soups, salads, and pasta. My favorite is her vegan lasagna. She also makes vegan pizza and delicious Mexican food.

As for eating out, you just have to be creative. Almost every restaurant has a cooler full of produce. A steakhouse has vegetables as sides, potatoes and salads. You may have to hold a few ingredients, but with a little thought, you can eat well. It is particularly easy eating meat-free and dairy-free in ethnic restaurants. Houston has several good vegan restaurants, including one that serves delicous Mexican food.

So many popular foods are available in vegan form that you could possibly become an overweight vegan. You are not doing yourself a favor if you replace your five-day-a-week burger-and-fries habit with a five-day-a-week veggie burger-and-fries habit. A veggie burger and fries or a vegan hot dog and onion rings are a nice occasional treat; however, you are not getting the full benefits of a plant-based diet. The true benefits come from eating a variety of fruits and vegetables in as close to their natural forms as you can. You will receive all the benefits of the vitamins, nutrients and minerals. Additionally, you will lose weight more easily because of caloric density.

The more processed food becomes, the higher its caloric density. For example, an average plain baked potato is 150 calories, which is the same amount of calories as twelve Lay's Stax chips. Which one will leave you full, and which one will fail to leave you full after you ingest the whole can (which is six servings and almost half the calories you need for the day)? Eating a can of Lay's Stax is like eating six baked potatoes. I have had a hard time finishing two baked potatoes as a meal. Not to mention, the baked potato is loaded with nutrients and the potato chip has little nutritional value.

For those of you who have decided that a plant-based diet is out of the question, cut down on meat and make smart choices. Instead of bacon and eggs for breakfast, have a bowl of steel-cut oats, almond milk, and fruit. For lunch, have a salad chock full of vegetables without a cream-based dressing. If you bring your lunch, enjoy the humble peanut butter and jelly sandwich and some fruit.

If you insist on eating meat, have a sanely sized piece of animal protein with dinner accompanied with a starch, vegetables, and salad. The more fruit and vegetables you eat, the better they will taste to you and the better you will feel and the better you will run. You will also notice that everything is easier when you hover around your ideal weight.

Other reasons besides your well-being for choosing a plant-based diet are eloquently stated in *Diet for a New America* by John Robbins. I heartily recommend this book and have said on numerous occasions that the book changed my life.

CHAPTER 19

In the past thirty years, I have learned a few things about running. Most of them were learned by good old trial and error. I hope that some of these things are beneficial and enhance your running experience. Like the significant changes in running, they are not listed in any particular order.

- Before you start an exercise program or reactivate an exercise regimen following a period of inactivity, get the okay from your doctor. It is important that you let your doctor know any symptoms you may be having. That is the time to tell your doctor about the pain in your chest after you climb a flight of stairs. Remember that being slim and trim does not necessarily guarantee you cardiac health or the level of fitness to participate in an exercise program.
- Get a complete physical once a year.
- A number of wonderful books will help you with your running program whether you are a beginner or the most seasoned runner. Make use of them. I am a big fan of Jeff Galloway's method because he considers running a lifetime activity, and everything is geared toward that instead of a single event. I run regularly with a fellow Galloway runner who just turned sixty-seven, and I have to ask him to slow down.

- Rest days are as every bit as important as running days. If you don't give your body a chance to recover, you are going to end up injured.

- On the rare occasion that you are too tired to get out of bed to run, you will not hurt anything by sleeping in. You probably need the rest.

- If you have a fever, don't run.

- Remember: neck and up, green light; below the neck, red. If you have a sore throat or a runny nose, you are good to run because they are neck-and-up maladies. If you have a cough that racks your chest or lower gastrointestinal distress, which are below-the-neck problems, you should stay in. Use common sense; most runners know when they are too sick to run.

- If you may be contagious, stay home or run alone. Do not share your misery with your running group or running partner. In fact, it may be a good day to stay in.

- Picking a regular time to run will give you the maximum time to recover and allow you to adjust your schedule accordingly. Early mornings work best for me. As a lawyer and a parent, I have no other guaranteed personal time until late at night. If a new client wants to meet in the evening or my children need help with homework (or have Daddy stare at the assignment befuddled as well), my run becomes a lower priority. Thanks to my overworked wife, my only demand in the morning is walking out the door with one of the children properly dressed by 7:20. I take full advantage of that luxury.

- Let someone know where you are going and how long you will be gone. If at all possible, indicate where you are going. Unfortunately, bad things can happen on a run, and in the event that they do, you want to be discovered as soon as possible.

- Carry identification. Additionally, if there is any information first responders need to know about you, have that information available as well. I personally prefer the Road ID bracelet and became much better about wearing it after an acquaintance was hit and killed on an early morning run and could not be identified for hours because of lack of identification.

- Know the difference between a twinge and pain. A twinge is mildly unpleasant and should resolve in short order. Anything else is pain, and you should stop or slow down to a walk immediately. I have made almost every one of my injuries worse by mentally dismissing it and continuing my run. Do not follow my example in this regard.

- In the event of an injury, walk if it is allowed. Even though it takes more time, you will maintain a superior level of fitness by walking. After an injury, you have to ease back into running. You will not be able to resume running at your same level and intensity. One year, while recovering from an injury, I was able to participate in meaningful marathon preparation by walking long distances with an occasional five- or ten-second running interval. It was long and tedious, but it was what I had to do to stay active and on target for the marathon I wanted to run.

- In the event that you cannot run or walk, reduce your calorie intake immediately from the calories you were burning when you were active. If you are running twenty miles per week, you are burning an extra two thousand calories per week by exercising. If you stop exercising, you have to compensate by eating less. If you do not, you will gain weight, which will usually exacerbate your injury and slow your recovery.

- If you cannot walk or run, look at viable cross-training activities, such as cycling, swimming, or jogging in a pool.

- When you are running, assume that bicyclists, motorcyclists, drivers, fellow runners, and walkers do not see you. Run defensively. I have a theory that motorcyclists are the safest runners since they assume that everyone is going to hit them. Do not rely on just one sense for your safety. You can no longer hear certain cars, and I can only assume that it would be just as unpleasant to be run over by a hybrid as it would to be run over by its less fuel-efficient counterpart.

- One of the few books on running I did not care for had the best advice about what to wear while running. Wear clothes that will allow you to be seen. It never occurred to me that my standard black shorts and black shirt could prevent a driver from seeing me on my morning run.

- If a fellow runner waves or gives you a good morning, reciprocate the friendly gesture. Everybody likes being acknowledged.

- If you are running in a group or a longer distance, carry a phone. The more people that you have running and the further the distance, the higher the probability of something going wrong, even if it is something as small as one runner having to walk the last five miles. Make the proper calls to let important people know that the schedule is off.

- If you are in a group and a runner has to walk the rest of the way, have someone walk it in with that runner unless you are absolutely sure the runner is strong enough to finish. Know where the runner is—and be sure he or she is in a safe area.

- On anything beyond your usual morning run, carry money. You never know when you will need a cab or emergency hydration. On a long summer run, the SAG wagon failed to show and if we hadn't brought money for drinks, it would have been a bad situation.

- Alcohol diminishes your tolerance to the heat. A long summer run after an alcohol-fueled bender is not a very good idea. Share that bottle of wine on the evening before an off day.

- Increase your mileage slowly. Most experts agree that a 10 percent increase per week is a safe amount. A more cautious amount would be 10 percent every two weeks. Increasing your mileage too fast increases the odds of an injury.

- Let your running clothes dry before you put them in with other laundry. Besides fabric softener, two common enemies of technical fabric are bra clasps and Velcro. Like the Capulets and the Montagues, nothing good is going to happen when they get together.

- If you wear glasses, keep something dry to clean them in the car. Following an unanticipated run in the rain, I went to drive home and had nothing to clean my glasses with. The story is protracted and messy, but the end result was nobody was hurt—and I was grateful my car had emergency roadside service. Learn from my very expensive mistake.

- Do not wear your marathon finisher shirt to a family run or a turkey trot.

- Before you go out for a run, sit for a few moments and make sure you have tended to your bodily functions. Nothing will take the joy out of a run faster than the call of nature without a bathroom in sight.

- On rare occasions, runners may burp or their bodies may make some other sounds that everyone but my wife makes. There is never any need to call it to their attention; they were aware of it before you were. In this regard, sugar-free items are not the foods to consume the night before a run.

- Thank every volunteer you can in a race. Imagine having to get up in the middle of the night to drive to a strange area to hand out packets or being driven to an isolated area to keep the toilet paper full in port-o-potties, stand guard over bags of clothing, yell out times, hand out cups of water, have water spilled on you, pick up paper cups, empty goo wrappers and sweaty clothing or offer first aid. This is just a small sampling of the tasks volunteers assume so you can enjoy your race safely. Dropping to your knees and kissing their hands would be commensurate with their efforts, but a mere heartfelt thank you should be your pleasure.

- Take the opportunity to volunteer at a race. You will be dropping to your knees in front of every volunteer during your next race.

- If you are having a bad run, it is an isolated incident. Your next run will always be better.
- Be flexible. If your group sets out to run ten miles, and the majority of the group wants to run less, keep the disappointment to yourself. If you are out by yourself on a ten-miler and start to feel poor, wind it down. Conversely, if you are out and you feel that you can run forever, put in an extra mile or two if you have the time. An isolated increase or decrease in mileage will not knock the earth off its axis. No training program is carved in stone.
- If you are going to run a particular race, tell everyone you know that you are going to do it. You will not be able to quit your training so easily.
- Everyone needs encouragement.
- It does not hurt to take time off from running after a long race. On the other hand, it will not hurt you to take a walk the following morning.
- An educated runner is a better runner. Read as much as you can about running.
- Sleeping in compression socks following a long race makes your legs feel much better in the morning. In fact, when I remember to do this, I can even walk normally the next day following a marathon. Well, almost normally.
- Nutrition is everything. It amazes me that people will read the owner's manual of their car but never take a moment to learn about what is best for optimal well-being. I have very strong feelings about this. Educate yourself about nutrition and what fuels are the best for you. Read more than trendy diet books. If we look at ourselves like our cars, we will recognize the fuels that keep us running optimally, the fuels that will cause temporary problems, and the fuels that can do permanent damage. If you are going to do it for your car, you can certainly do it for yourself.

- Before a long run (more than ten miles), I eat a Nature's Path Toaster Pastry. They are every bit as processed as a regular Pop Tart, but the ingredients are healthier and easy to digest. For about 210 calories, you get 40 grams of carbohydrates. A Clif Bar has almost the same nutritional value and works equally well.
- I have an unusual prerace meal. While the marathoning world eats pasta, I prefer a vegetable pizza without the cheese. My all-time favorite, despite the fact that their crust is not pure vegan, is the Joe's Pizza at Star Pizza in Houston. The Joe's is sautéed spinach with fresh garlic. I have them add onions and sliced Kalamata olives. It has not failed me yet. My second favorite is the primavera at Collina's in Houston, holding the squash and zucchini because I hate them. That pie has always worked for me as well.
- Recycle and donate. I am through with running shoes after three hundred miles and I am lucky to get three months out of them. The shoes may no longer be suited for their intended purpose, but they still have lots of life. Since I use Superfeet insoles in my shoes, I remove and save the original insoles from the shoes the minute I get the shoe home. When I am done with the shoes, I wash them in the machine, put in the original insoles (they look brand new), and donate them so they get a second chance to be useful. Additionally, I donate most of the shirts I receive from races since I have enough or will never wear them. I hope that race sponsors decide to give us the option of taking the shirt, donating the shirt, or giving the value of the shirt to someone in need.
- Always give yourself time to walk before a run and time to walk after. It gives your body a chance to warm up and cool down.
- If you have to drive to an area to run instead of being able to take off from your front door, invest in a seat cover to keep from ruining your seats and to ensure that they will be dry the next time you get in the car. I have found that the terrycloth ones, albeit more attractive, do not work as well as the ones made out

of technical fabric. After my run, I put on an old hoody so my running clothes will not soak the safety belt.

- It never hurts to run in a light rain; however, never run when there is lightning. You can run in a harder rain, but consider that visibility is limited both ways. You have difficulty seeing things, and cars cannot see you.

- Even though I am the worst about this, go to the gym on your off days. Any work you can do on your core will improve your running form. To further improve or maintain your running form, the hip abduction/adduction machine is helpful as well. Another favorite machine is the one that works out your Achilles. The Achilles is often overlooked to strengthen, which is a mistake. Any injury to the Achilles is slow to heal because of the relatively low blood flow in the muscle. If you are serious about distance running, your goal is to stay firm without bulking up. Since muscle is heavier than fat, the less you are carrying over a long distance, the better.

- Keep a running log. Many commercial running logs are available. None of them are state of the art so you can even custom make one to keep track of what is important to you. Most logs will allow you to record distance, time, and speed, and they generally have a place to note how you are feeling. Some people keep track of their pulse rate. In my neurotic fashion, I keep track of the miles I have on a particular shoe.

- Keep a food log. People who keep food logs do a better job maintaining their ideal weights. You can compare it to your running log and determine what foods work best for your running.

- Roll on your foam roller at least twice a day. I believe that the more you roll, the less likely you are to sustain an injury. If a therapist or any other health care provider has given you particular stretches to do, do them as prescribed.

- Do not run on antihistamines or any other drug whose purpose is to dry you out. As explained earlier, hydration is an important part of running. Running on a medication that dehydrates you can lead to heat-related maladies and muscle injuries. If you have any question about whether to exercise on a certain drug, ask your physician or pharmacist.

- Never put your running shoes in the washing machine unless they are retired from running. If they are wet, let them dry outside (out of direct sunlight). Also, if they are drying, it may not be a bad idea to remove the insole. Finally, if a shoe becomes so dirty or odiferous that you cannot stand it anymore, it will not hurt a shoe to turn a hose on it. I do this on rare occasions, but I use the least amount of water possible.

This list is hardly exclusive. These are just common sense tips I have picked up over the years and I hope they will make your running a little better.

CHAPTER 20

Running has been such a major part of my life for such a long time. This writing experience stirred up memories that have been dormant for many years, and I was glad to revisit them.

It is hard to put my finger on why running has been such a major part of my life. It is not the most important thing in my life. Those would be my wife and children. It has never provided for my family. To the contrary, with the price of shoes and gear, running can be relatively expensive. I can say that if I could compare running to my chosen profession, finishing a marathon is akin to winning a trial. For that moment—and in the days that follow—all is well in the universe. Also, as far as both undertakings go, the better shape you in are going into it, the better you will be coming out of it.

Running has changed my life dramatically. After being an obese teenager with poor eating habits and a very uncertain future, running gave me the self-esteem to better myself and run away from my former fat self. Sometimes my former fat self starts to gain on me, but I know what I have to do to lose him. I will go for a run, and he will fall behind. I do not see him regularly, but I know he is still out there. Once in a blue moon, I think I see him when I am looking in a mirror, but I stare—and he goes away.

Besides improving the quality of my life, I believe that running has added years to my life. Obesity, inactivity, and a fast-food diet are not factors that lead to length of days. It is not a stretch to believe I would not have seen fifty at that rate I was going.

I have met wonderful people running. Our paths have changed, literally and figuratively, but we have had wonderful conversations and better runs that sustain me to this day. I will never forget going home to St. Louis for the holidays after my first semester of law school. I went for a run with Coach Carr, a gym teacher who taught at my high school. It had been just over four years since he saw a fat kid graduate, and now that same young man was running with him in the snow, stride for stride for six miles. His two-word "good run" was the delayed stamp of approval that eluded me throughout my formative school years.

Roger Moore, "like James Bond" as he used to say, would shout words of encouragement to runners in Memorial Park. On rare occasions, we would run together, and he would always push me further than I thought I could go. The years went by, and I saw him walking. When I didn't see him anymore, I remembered that the ability to run and life are gifts that do not last forever.

As I get older, I look forward to every run. I am fortunate that I am not plagued by a lack of motivation in this area. Maybe I can sense there are fewer runs ahead of me than behind me. Even though I hope not, that is reality. I hope that I will be running in my eighties, but more likely than not, there will be a day when I decide that is the last run—and then I will walk and then those days will come to an end. It will not be a sad day. I have enjoyed almost every mile I covered, and I realize what a blessing it was to be able to do so.

My oldest daughter runs track. Unlike me, she is actually fast and has no desire to run distance. During the 2012 Houston Marathon, my youngest daughter was lowered onto the course, held my hand, and ran the last yards of the race with me. I hope that she someday crosses a marathon finishing line on her own.

When you get right down to it, I just love running. I know what my life was without it—and I know what my life is like with it. It has made me a better person.

When I first thought about writing a book, it struck me that in thirty-three years, more than 7,500 runs and more than 35,000 miles, there has only been one time I have not finished my run in the same place I started. I have spent my whole life running in circles, and I will continue to do so because it agrees with me.

POSTSCRIPT

I was looking forward to Thanksgiving 2012. Some of my wife's family was coming to visit us, and I was hoping to spend time with family, catch up on my sleep and pleasure reading, and see a few movies, which is one of my all-time favorite activities. On the Wednesday before Thanksgiving, I had a perfect run. I got to sleep late because I did not have court that morning, and I met my friends Denise and Carole for an easy six miles.

Family rolled in throughout the day. After dinner, my brother-in-law and I went upstairs to watch a movie. Toward the end of the movie, my throat started feeling sore and my nose was running. Immediately following the credits, I was in bed suffering from my earlier symptoms and feeling achy. I spent the weekend in bed and went to the doctor on Monday. I was given antibiotics and something to clear my chest, which had become congested. By that time, I had myself worked up into a complete snit believing that I was too sick to run the 50K in Huntsville that weekend.

I took the medication until Thursday and thought that I was probably good to go. Since it was tapering time, I did three on that same day and felt good but not great. I believed that if I could get in two good nights of sleep, I would be fine by Saturday. On Friday night, I laid out my gear, ate my Joe's Pizza at Star Pizza, and felt ready to go.

I had run the race many times, and the temperatures ranged from freezing to blistering hot. As it turned out, this was going to be a very warm December day, particularly for running. The race was broken down into one 6 mile loop and two 12½-mile loops. A group of us stuck together the first lap, and for such a short distance, I was sweating profusely. I was kicking myself for not stopping at the first water stop and drinking.

I finished the first lap, immediately downed some fluids, and took off. I finished the second loop, but at mile seventeen or so, the proverbial wheels were falling off the wagon. I was hot, tired, and had a difficult time maintaining anything that resembled running. I was thinking of turning it in after the second lap. I started to talk to a group of women who had started the race with me, and we were taking turns passing each other.

As it turned out, one of the women in the group had run the race as many times as I had and was feeling the exact same way I was. Her determination to finish the race even if she had to crawl turned out to be contagious. They were kind enough to let me join them for the final lap. As it turned out, keeping up with their reduced clip was a tad optimistic on my part. I started to fall behind at mile twenty-two or twenty-three. As good fortune would have it, two women had been reduced to a brisk walking pace, and I fell in with them. With nine more of ten miles to the finish, their company was welcome and took my mind off my misery and my worst race performance ever. With approximately half a mile to go, they picked up the pace, leaving me to finish the race at my own pace.

As I approached the finish line, Roger Soler urged me to pick up the pace. I could not. I was completely exhausted. I said my good-byes, got in the car, and drove home. On the way home, I called two friends who were going to run the race with me and shared my disappointing outing with them. By that time, I had resolved to cancel my subscription to *Trail Runner* magazine and donate my trail shoes.

I took the next four days off and went for an easy four-mile run the next Thursday. My legs felt great. I had reassessed the last race and was feeling completely different about things. Mostly, I was grateful to my fellow runners who were so encouraging and took me in when I was having such a rough time. Thinking of how beautiful the course was helped a bit. The bottom line was that I *did* finish the race. It just happened to be harder than I thought, and the ending was not as pretty as I would have liked.

My experience in Huntsville and the footage of the marathoners deprived of their marathon in New York helping the victims of Hurricane Sandy caused me to think about human kindness. Basically, a small random act of kindness or compassion could affect someone's life for a moment or forever. In retrospect, that is what Byron Woods did for me. Before I began running, I was heavy, physically uncomfortable, and I hated what I saw in the mirror. I was confined by misery and self-loathing; my world was self-contained. My isolation, whether actual or created by my poor self-esteem, affected my social growth. That is the cruelest consequence of childhood obesity.

Even as my body changed, the fat old me kept staring back at me every morning. As the years went on, I actually had a handful of good mirror days. I was trying to catch up with where I should have been. Even though I looked normal on the outside, it was like I had been placed in college with only a third-grade education. I was determined to overcome the social handicap that obesity had on my life, and I think I have done so. I see fat Rand less and less, and when he begins to hang around, I can still outrun him.

Generally speaking, no other community offers more unconditional support than the running community. I owe it a debt of gratitude for always supporting me—and everyone else who has ever put on a pair of running shoes. I cannot end this book with just one wish for every runner because there is a universal wish: I wish you injury-free running. But taking that one out of the equation, my wish would be the following: May you always receive a kind or encouraging word when the road is looking it's roughest—and may you always respond to your fellow runners in kind.

ABOUT THE AUTHOR

Rand Mintzer is a practicing criminal defense attorney. He was born in St. Louis, Missouri, and was educated at Arkansas State University and South Texas College of Law. He lives in Houston with his wife Andrea and their daughters, Avery and Hayden.